Building Greener Neighborhoods

Trees as Part of the Plan

Jack Petit
AMERICAN FORESTS

Debra L. Bassert
National Association of Home Builders

Cheryl Kollin
AMERICAN FORESTS

Published jointly by
AMERICAN FORESTS and
Home Builder Press, National Association of Home Builders

AMERICAN FORESTS
P.O. Box 2000
Washington, DC 20013-2000
(202) 667-3300

Home Builder Press®
National Association of Home Builders
1201 15th Street, NW
Washington, DC 20005-2800
(800) 223-2665

This publication is designed to provide accurate and authoritative information in regard to the subject matter covered. It is sold with the understanding that the publisher is not engaged in rendering legal, accounting, or other professional service. If legal advice or other expert assistance is required, the services of a competent professional person should be sought.

—From a Declaration of Principles jointly adopted by a Committee of the American Bar Association and a Committee of Publishers and Associations.

Building Greener Neighborhoods: Trees as Part of the Plan
ISBN 0-86718-409-4

© 1995 by AMERICAN FORESTS and Home Builder Press® of the National Association of Home Builders of the United States of America

Cover photo by Mark Finkenstaedt. Wyndcrest, Sandy Spring, Maryland, Joseph Alfandre Homebuilding.

Printed in the United States of America on recycled paper

Library of Congress Cataloging-in-Publication Data

Petit, Jack.
   Building greener neighborhoods : trees as part of the plan / Jack Petit, Debra L. Bassert (National Association of Home Builders), Cheryl Kollin (American Forests).
      p.   cm.
   Includes bibliographical references (p.   ).
   ISBN 0-86718-409-4 (alk. paper)
   1. Ornamental trees. 2. Trees in cities. 3. Building sites—Planning. 4. Ornamental trees—United States. 5. Trees in cities—United States. 6. Building sites—United States—Planning.
   I. Bassert, Debra L. II. Kollin, Cheryl. III. American Forests (Association) IV. National Association of Home Builders (U.S.) V. Title.
   SB435.5.P48   1995
   715'.2—dc20   95-23613
                                                                CIP

For further information, please contact—

AMERICAN FORESTS
P.O. Box 2000
Washington, DC 20013-2000
(202) 667-3300

Home Builder Press®
National Association of Home Builders
1201 15th Street, NW
Washington, DC 20005-2800
(800) 223-2665

8/95 Home Builder Press/DataReproductions 2,500

Contents

About the Authors

AMERICAN FORESTS, founded in 1875, is this country's oldest national citizen conservation organization. Its mission is to communicate the many benefits of trees and forests in both rural and urban areas. Long known for its tireless efforts toward the creation of national forests and parks, the former American Forestry Association is now the leading voice for urban forests. Using state-of-the-art computer technology, sound science, and good sense, AMERICAN FORESTS is showing professional and lay leaders the value of the nation's urban forests for energy savings, the functioning of ecosystems, and increased home values. AMERICAN FORESTS produces a wide variety of both technical and easy-to-read publications, ranging from award-winning magazines and the National Register of Big Trees to books and brochures on tree planting and care.

Founded in 1942, the National Association of Home Builders (NAHB) is the trade association for the home building industry. As a federation of more than 800 state and local associations, NAHB's mission is to enhance the climate for home building and to promote policies that keep housing a national priority. The association has more than 180,000 members, including home builders, developers, multifamily and commercial builders, remodelers, and a broad spectrum of professionals who support the industry. Through its many educational programs and publications, NAHB provides members and associations the latest information on construction, business management, land development, sales and marketing, economics, finance, legislation, government regulations, consumer attitudes and preferences, and other specialized fields within the housing industry.

Jack Petit is a former Urban Forestry Associate for AMERICAN FORESTS. He served as Program Coordinator for Global ReLeaf for New Communities, contributed articles to *Urban Forests* magazine, and managed public correspondence on urban forestry issues. While working on this book, Mr. Petit interviewed many of the developers cited. A horticulturalist specializing in tropical and subtropical plants, Mr. Petit is currently working on a series of gardening booklets for the northern Gulf Coast. He resides in Mobile, Alabama.

Debra L. Bassert is the Senior Land Use Planner in the Land Development Services department of the National Association of Home Builders and has 13 years of experience in land use planning. She provides technical assistance on a wide range of land use planning and development issues; reviews and provides detailed comments on local comprehensive plans, zoning and subdivision regulations, and special purpose ordinance provisions, including tree protection requirements; is Assistant Editor of NAHB's *Land Development* magazine; and manages NAHB's joint role in the Global ReLeaf for New Communities recognition program. Prior to joining NAHB's staff, she worked in local government and for a private consulting firm. Ms. Bassert holds a Bachelor of Arts in Economics from Bryn Mawr College and a master's degree in Urban and Environmental Planning from the School of Architecture at the University of Virginia.

Cheryl Kollin serves as Director of Urban Forestry for AMERICAN FORESTS. She is a landscape architect and certified arborist with more than 10 years' experience in the field of urban forestry in the public, private, and nonprofit sectors. Ms. Kollin provides applied urban forestry research to cost-benefit studies, land and housing development, tree health issues, and energy conservation; provides technical guidance for the Global ReLeaf for New Communities recognition program, reviewing development submittals and natural resource expert applications; and contributes to *Urban Forests* magazine and other AMERICAN FORESTS publications. Ms. Kollin holds a bachelor's degree in Natural Resource Science from the University of Michigan and a master's degree in Landscape Architecture from the University of California-Berkeley.

Acknowledgments

This book is the result of an extraordinary collaboration between home builders and conservationists. Our first thanks go to Maryland developer Michael T. Rose (whose preface follows this text) and urban forester Steve Clark for introducing the National Association of Home Builders and AMERICAN FORESTS to each other and for contributing so many of the ideas in this book based on their years of experience building with nature.

AMERICAN FORESTS' Vice President for Urban Forestry, Gary Moll, and NAHB's Joseph R. Molinaro, Director, Land Development Services, and Debra L. Bassert, Senior Land Use Planner, deserve the lion's share of the credit for getting their respective organizations to create Global ReLeaf for New Communities, the recognition program for developers and builders, which led to the writing of this book. Their willingness to seek common ground has exemplified the spirit needed to provide America with homes while conserving the natural environment.

Thanks also to our responsive reviewers—developers, builders, and landscape architects—who verified that the techniques and information presented in this book accurately reflect those used out in the field: David S. Ager, Rodgers and Associates, Inc., Gaithersburg, Maryland; William G. Boyer, Boyer Custom Homes, Schertz, Texas; Mary Ann Lasch, LBI-HOK, Doha, Qatar; Gary Moll, AMERICAN FORESTS, Washington, DC; Michael T. Rose and S. Robert Kaufman, Michael T. Rose Companies, Laurel, Maryland; Darrel L. Seibert, Seibert Development Corporation, Stow, Ohio; Michael F. Shibley, NAHB Staff Vice President, Washington, DC; Ronald A. Stupp, Ron Stupp Associates, Ellicott City, Maryland; and David T. Yost, Future Investments Company, Oklahoma City, Oklahoma.

Special thanks must also go to the urban forestry and development industry pioneers who found ways to build around trees and shared their success stories with us for this book: Charles Stewart, Urban Forest Management, Inc., Fox River Grove, Illinois; James Clark, HortScience, Inc., Pleasanton, California; Steve W. Clark,

Steve Clark, Inc., Natural Resource Planner/Urban Forester, Brentwood, Tennessee; Robert Birchell, Robert Birchell and Associates, Oklahoma City, Oklahoma; Michael Stadulis, Realen Homes, Ambler, Pennsylvania; Brittons' Tree Service, Sacramento, California; Bray McDonald, County Agent's Assistant, Mobile, Alabama; Michael T. Rose, Michael T. Rose Companies, Laurel, Maryland; David T. Yost, Future Investments Company, Oklahoma City, Oklahoma; C.P. Morgan and Mark W. Boyce, C.P. Morgan Company, Inc., Carmel, Indiana; Bradley B. Chambers, The Buckingham Companies, Indianapolis, Indiana; G. David Gale, F.E.L. Lands, Santa Barbara, California; Roger B. Gatewood, Westfield Development Corporation, Oldsmar, Florida; and United Parcel Service, Atlanta, Georgia. Thanks to all of them for taking the risk of breaking new ground.

Many other talented people nurtured this book in its early stages, especially former AMERICAN FORESTS staffers Phillip Rodbell and Jeff Pappas. AMERICAN FORESTS Managing Editor Michelle Robbins pared down and refined the voluminous drafts of this text with skill and sensitivity, making it a better read for all. AMERICAN FORESTS' Linda Mallet assisted with checking final details and logistics. At NAHB, Michaela Birstad and Susan O'Connor cheerfully word processed the many text changes under tight deadlines.

Finally, we would like to acknowledge the NAHB Home Builder Press staff for their interest in seeing this book published and their work getting it into print: Rosanne O'Connor, Director of Publications, whose editorial guidance helped make this book possible; Adrienne Ash, Assistant Staff Vice President, Information and Publication Services; Julie Wilson, Director of Sales and Marketing; Bo O'Dea, Publications Sales Manager; Stephanie Thomas, Manager, Home Builder Bookstore; John Tuttle, Publications Editor; Carolyn Kamara, Editorial Assistant; and David Rhodes, Art and Production Director.

This book was produced under the general direction of Neil Sampson, AMERICAN FORESTS Executive Vice President; Kent W. Colton, NAHB Executive Vice President and CEO; Bob Brown, NAHB Senior Staff Vice President, State, Local, and Regulatory Affairs Division; and James DeLizia, NAHB Staff Vice President, Member and Association Relations Division.

Preface

Why did the National Association of Home Builders and
AMERICAN FORESTS, a citizen conservation organization, team
up to write a book about trees? The reason for this book and the
unique collaboration that brought it about is to show those involved
in building new communities the advantages of saving, planting,
and transplanting more trees in their developments and the rewards
of doing so. The book is about sharing information, working together toward common goals, and creating a win-win situation
for everyone involved, especially for the communities in which we
all live.

With the information in this book, builders and developers can
make it possible for homeowners in newly built communities to en-
joy mature trees and natural areas close to home. The book explains
how to select which trees to save, plant, or transplant to comple-
ment the developed areas of a site; how to minimize disturbance to
trees slated for protection; and how to select trees for removal,
either to enhance other, more desirable trees or to make way for
buildings, roads, and other constructed areas of a site. It also describes how creating a tree conservation plan to guide land planning
and work with existing topography can reduce development costs;
how conserving trees will enhance the appeal of a development and
help it compete more effectively for sales with older, more established neighborhoods; how developers and builders can earn recognition for their tree conservation efforts; and how they can
publicize their distinctive communities through advertising, brochures, signage, and other techniques.

Successful tree conservation requires a shared vision and a commitment from developers, government officials, and local communities *to work together* and to acknowledge the challenges developers
and builders face. Many regulations have a built-in conflict between saving trees and developing land. When local grading laws
require three-to-one instead of two-to-one slopes or a 20-foot ledge
of cleared area around homes, this means that the developer must
clear more trees. When road standards require 32 feet of pavement

when 24 will do, this mandates yet more clearing. If developers must construct large stormwater management ponds when sheet flow on wooded sites would work just as well, even fewer trees will remain. Many communities prescribe development standards based on a single focus and often do not consider the impact of one regulation on another.

This book contains real-world examples, drawn from decades of experience on the part of home builders, land developers, and urban foresters working in partnership with local government. These success stories show how saving mature trees and contiguous forests requires coordinated planning and local government approval of innovative land-planning techniques such as cluster development, where lots are made smaller (but density is not increased) so that more open space can be preserved for everyone's use and benefit. Public officials who understand the benefit of waiving the rules to save more trees and who realize that regulatory flexibility will not jeopardize the health, safety, or welfare of a community's residents can help developers save more trees. Officials and citizens who acknowledge the principles of tree conservation understand this means blending development with the land and recognize the necessity to remove some trees during development to make room for homes, roads, ballfields, tot lots, lakes, stormwater management, and utilities.

Success in conserving trees involves planning, cooperation, communication, and commitment among the many members of the development team as well—site engineers, land planners, attorneys, urban foresters, builders, subcontractors, landscape architects, and others. An early investment in planning and management will reap rewards for the developer and builder not just in terms of protected trees, but also in the form of more marketable projects. As team leader, the developer must work hard to educate the rest of the development team about project goals and to carefully plan and implement tree conservation strategies with other team members throughout the approval, development, and construction processes. Once a new community is completed, the developer must convey responsibility for ongoing maintenance of the new community's trees to the new homeowners, the homeowners' association, and the local government.

In spite of the many obstacles, developers and builders should approach every new plan with the attitude that it can be done. This means involving the public early, possibly building nontraditional coalitions with environmental groups, civic or neighborhood associations, or others who may share similar goals. It almost always means showing local officials how they can help make better communities possible by allowing the development team flexibility to respond creatively to the unique possibilities of each site.

Communities are created by developers and builders—they don't just happen by themselves. Builders and developers take pride in the new homes, communities, and urban forests that we all live in. But the building industry is constantly working to improve its techniques and successes. Hopefully, this book will offer some new ideas on how to conserve trees in developments, reducing costs in the process and enhancing both the value of new homes and neighborhoods for homeowners and the quality of their lives.

Keep in mind that removing trees costs money, and that home buyers and renters across the board appreciate homes with trees and will pay more for them—whether it's single-family detached homes on large lots, small homes for empty nesters, townhomes, or multifamily dwellings. Conserving trees is not an easy task, but in our experience it's worth doing.

—Michael T. Rose
Communities That Live With Nature
May 1995

Chapter 1

Introduction

Today's home buyers are increasingly interested not only in the interior of their new home but also in its surroundings (see Figure 1.1). More than half of 1,350 real estate agents surveyed in 1994 by Bank America Mortgage thought trees had a positive impact on potential buyers' impressions of both a home and a neighborhood. Eighty-four percent believed that a home with trees would be as much as 20 percent more salable in terms of property value and curb appeal than a similar, treeless home.

Surveys confirm the home-buying public's interest in seeing more trees saved and planted around homes. In 1993, the National Association of Home Builders (NAHB) polled 1,000 homeowners on how builders can help the environment; 89 percent advised them to leave as many trees as possible, while 77 percent said builders should add more trees to developments. A recent NAHB survey of builders found that people are also willing to pay more for homes with trees: Builders reported that 43 percent of home buyers paid up to $3,000 more, 30 percent paid between $3,000 and $5,000 more, and 27 percent spent over $5,000 more—with 8 percent of those spending an additional $10,000—for wooded lots.

Across the country, in good times and bad, properties with saved and transplanted trees have proven to sell or rent faster and better than properties without trees. But other benefits also accrue from conserving trees. Tree conservation can save builders and developers money that would have been spent on clearing, grading, and landscaping; help a developer meet erosion control and storm-water management requirements in a more cost-effective way; and

1.1 *A well-treed lot adds buyer appeal to a home.*

Source: Williamsburg Commons, Cary, North Carolina. Design by William E. Poole Design, Inc. Photograph by Tim R. Newell.

provide distinctive, marketable amenities that set new homes and neighborhoods apart from the competition. The attractive results of tree conservation efforts pay off further by helping developers and builders secure a more positive reputation with local officials and the public for doing quality projects, which can make approvals on future projects easier to obtain. (Throughout the book, "tree conservation" refers to saving, planting, and transplanting trees.)

Successful tree conservation does require careful project planning, supervision, and construction practices, and it can mean working to obtain waivers or exemptions from local regulatory requirements. However, retaining existing, mature trees on a site can offer greater benefits aesthetically, environmentally, and economically than typical landscaping.

In spite of these trends, little has been written for developers and builders on the benefits trees offer. Even less has been written to guide developers and builders on how to conserve trees while developing property. Developers, builders, engineers, and public policymakers have had virtually nowhere to turn for an understanding of how best to incorporate tree conservation into the development process.

This book sets out to demonstrate how to use a site's existing tree resources to their best advantage and how to incorporate tree conservation goals into project planning and construction in a cost-effective manner. Chapter 2 describes the benefits of trees—including many economic benefits only recently quantified by research. Chapter 3 examines the physiology of trees, with an emphasis on how development and construction activities affect them. Chapter 4 discusses how to plan for trees in preparing to develop a site and introduces the natural resource expert to the development team—a professional whose insights improve the chances for success in blending tree conservation and construction activity.

Chapter 5 discusses how to train, educate, and supervise members of the development and construction team to minimize construction impacts and to protect the team's efforts over the long term once homes are sold. The sixth and final chapter details how to market successes in building with trees and highlights AMERICAN FORESTS' and NAHB's Global ReLeaf for New Communities recognition program for builders and developers. (For information on enrolling in this program, see AMERICAN FORESTS' listing in the Appendix.)

Until now, few professionals had a working knowledge of both land development and environmental processes. Developers seeking approvals for new projects too often faced angry citizens frustrated over the loss of trees in their communities. By presenting the latest urban forestry information as it relates to the land development business, this book shows how to realize everyone's tree goals in a more productive and harmonious manner. As developers and builders who have pioneered such efforts have already discovered, the results benefit everyone—aesthetically, politically, and economically. This book will show you that it is possible to have houses *and* the environment.

Chapter 2

Benefits of Trees

Trees shade our homes, give our children a place to play, and provide fuel and lumber. But they do more than that. Trees reduce soil erosion, improve air quality, shield us from solar radiation, and filter and reduce stormwater runoff. Today, the field of urban forestry is identifying these broader benefits that may be less obvious to the uninitiated.

This chapter will explore the value of trees, beginning with the broader benefits they bring to the urban ecosystem. Homeowners increasingly recognize that trees provide economic as well as environmental and aesthetic advantages, and they generally are willing to pay more for lots with trees. Through energy savings and other benefits, trees offer incentives that developers can use to produce a better product for the consumer, one that is in greater demand and therefore sells faster and commands a higher price. Figure 2.1 summarizes the benefits trees provide.

This chapter will also explore some of the innovative ways builders and developers increase their success by incorporating trees and natural elements into development sites. Trees can offer tangible financial returns through savings on clearing and landscaping expenses, enhanced marketing opportunities, and added value that translates to improved lot and home sales. They also offer intangible benefits such as an enhanced public image for the developer and a favorable reaction from local officials when the developer seeks regulatory approvals or concessions.

2.1 Benefits of Trees

Energy Conservation and Air Quality

- ◆ Deciduous trees provide shade and can save 10 to 50 percent on a home's summer cooling costs.
- ◆ Deciduous trees provide evaporative cooling, lowering temperatures throughout a community.
- ◆ Evergreen trees block winter winds and can save 20 percent on a home's winter heating needs.
- ◆ Trees store carbon, offsetting the harmful by-products of burning fossil fuels.
- ◆ Trees trap air pollution particulates, cleaning air.

Stormwater Control and Water Quality

- ◆ Trees intercept and absorb stormwater, reducing runoff and soil erosion.
- ◆ Tree buffers near waterways improve water quality by acting as a filter.

Psychological and Physical Health

- ◆ Trees have a restorative effect that can improve physical well-being.
- ◆ Trees block and mask noise.
- ◆ Trees offer beauty and create a sense of place in the community.
- ◆ Trees provide recreational settings and wildlife habitat.

Marketability

- ◆ A well-treed development enhances property values and sales.
- ◆ Tree conservation enhances the developer's and builder's image.

Energy Conservation

Direct Cooling

Trees provide enormous cooling benefits, principally through two mechanisms. First, because they absorb sunlight and offer shade, trees prevent sunlight from reaching surfaces such as concrete, brick, and asphalt that convert solar radiation into heat. Second, trees release water vapor through tiny openings in their leaves—a process known as evapotranspiration; the water vapor absorbs heat directly from the air and cools it. Evapotranspiration seems to be important not only in modifying extreme heat in yards and neighborhoods, but also for moderating regional and even global climates.

By lowering extreme temperatures, trees reduce the physical discomfort that people suffer in high heat. And trees reduce the need for energy to run air conditioners. In addition to reducing the actual bill for a business or homeowner, this reduction in energy usage cuts down on pollution produced by utilities.

The savings that homeowners can reap from well-placed trees range from 10 to 50 percent during the summer cooling season, based on computer-modeling studies by the Environmental Protection Agency (EPA) and the U.S. Forest Service. A developer who has strategically saved and/or planted trees can legitimately advertise a product as more energy-efficient than a comparable parcel or unit that has no trees or is inappropriately sited among its trees.

In a city like Tucson, Arizona, a single drought-tolerant tree planted strategically to save on cooling will conserve up to 300 kilowatt-hours (kWh) per year. By reducing the amount of electricity needed for air conditioning, the tree also reduces the amount of water needed for generating electricity—a savings of about 180 gallons annually per tree.

In her remarks at the Sixth National Urban Forest Conference, Minnesota landscape architect Peggy Sand highlighted five strategies for using trees to maximize energy savings for homes and businesses. Three dealt with cooling, two with heating.

First, "west is best" is a general rule of thumb when considering where to shade a building. In most climate zones, western exposures struck by the summer sun reach the hottest temperatures, adding considerably to the discomfort felt within a home and to the cost of cooling it (see Figure 2.2). However, in certain parts of the country, such as south Florida, research indicates that shading eastern exposures is just as important, because trees that shade both eastern and western walls will greatly reduce heat extremes in the summertime.

Strange as it may seem, shading a southern exposure is not as important as shading a western or eastern one. This is because the summer sun is usually high enough overhead at midday that the

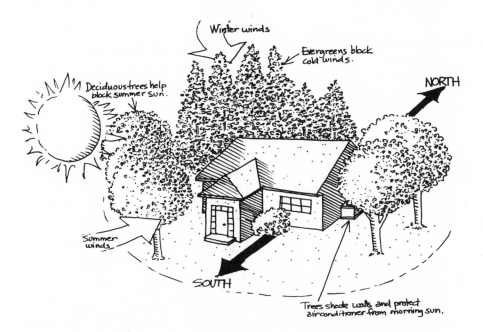

Winter winds

Evergreens block
cold winds.

Deciduous trees help
block summer sun.

NORTH

Summer
winds

SOUTH

Trees shade walls and protect
aircondioner from morning sun.

2.2 *For energy savings, plant deciduous trees to the east and west of a house and around air conditioners to create shade; plant evergreens to the north and west to block winter winds; and avoid plantings to the south.*

Source: Reprinted with permission from Bono Mitchell Graphics.

southern wall is shaded by eaves. Particularly in northern latitudes, trees on the south side of a home provide little energy savings in summer and can block important solar heating gains during winter.

The second important strategy is to shade the air conditioner or central heating/air-conditioning unit itself. This measure alone can cut 10 percent from a household's summer energy bill, since air conditioners are most effective and efficient when operating in a cooler environment. In the Sunbelt, air conditioners and central units should be shaded year-round. Maximum benefits accrue when small- to medium-sized trees, rather than shrubs, are used, offering a cool microclimate but allowing for good airflow to and from the unit. While waiting for trees to grow, homeowners can get immediate results by using shade cloth or fast-growing vines trained on trellises.

Indirect Cooling

The third strategy for maximizing trees' cooling benefits could be called "more is better." Groupings of trees provide significantly more atmospheric cooling than would be expected—a "sum greater than the parts."

The general atmospheric cooling of evapotranspiration is powerful—and important economically. This is because certain characteristics of urban areas raise the summer temperatures there higher than in surrounding rural areas. Communities contain large amounts of "low albedo" surfaces—surfaces such as pavement that absorb sunlight and convert it to heat. Cities also generate heat as a by-product of cars, lights, energy production, and industry—and tend to have less vegetation to offset this extra heat.

These factors tend to produce an "island" of warmer air over cities, resulting in temperatures that in this country are typically 5 to 9 degrees Fahrenheit warmer than the surrounding countryside. This is known as the "heat-island effect," and generally, the larger the city, the greater is the temperature difference (see Figure 2.3).

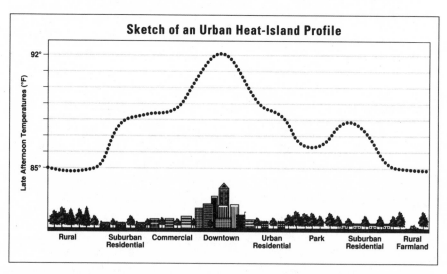

2.3 City summer temperatures are typically warmer than those in the surrounding suburban and rural countryside because of increased built area and human activity and decreased tree canopy, a phenomenon known as the "urban heat-island effect."

Source: H. Akbari, S. Davis, S. Dorsano, J. Huang, and S. Winnett (eds.), *Cooling Our Communities: A Guidebook on Tree Planting and Light-Colored Surfacing*, Doc. 22P-2001 (Washington, DC: U.S. Environmental Protection Agency, Office of Policy, Planning, and Evaluation, 1992), p. 217.

All trees help cool the air in hot weather through evapotranspiration, with larger trees having a greater impact. Similarly, groupings of trees have a greater cooling effect, as evidenced by the cooler temperatures felt in and immediately around city parks. By keeping the ground below them in shade, groups of trees preserve soil moisture and create cool microclimates. Grouped trees also buffer each other from the effects of heat and harsh climate, maintaining health in the stand and helping the trees cool the air more effectively. The bottom line? A community realizes greater cooling benefits from trees in groups than from the same number of evenly spaced, isolated trees.

How much of a difference can trees make for a community? Researcher Hashem Akbari of the University of California's Lawrence Berkeley Laboratory (LBL) has studied urban energy usage and the heat-island effect for years. He estimates that the heat-island effect alone costs Washington, DC, some $40,000 per hour during the summer. For Los Angeles, that figure soars to $150,000 per hour.

In 1993-94, AMERICAN FORESTS used sophisticated computer technology to conduct a detailed analysis of the city of Frederick, Maryland (population 40,000). AMERICAN FORESTS examined the cooling benefits the city receives from its existing trees and discovered that Frederick's trees save residents an average of almost $1 million per year in energy costs alone. Even more significant, the study found that strategically placed trees could save the city another $2 million in direct energy use savings annually. In addition, other research shows that indirect savings are equal to direct savings, doubling the overall amount saved to $6 million.

Similarly, in a study of the newly developed Whittier neighborhood in Frederick, AMERICAN FORESTS examined the cooling benefits provided by existing trees. The trees currently growing in the Whittier development were found to save approximately $23 per building at maturity. When the same trees were strategically sited using computer modeling, the projected savings increased to $100 per building.

For builders and developers, these studies indicate how a good product can be made better, not only for the consumer buying it but for the community in which it is built.

Winter Heating

The two remaining energy-saving strategies concern the heat-conserving benefits trees provide during winter.

The first strategy is to "let the sun shine in." In winter, passive solar radiation entering through windows can provide free heating—up to 20 percent of a home's heating needs. Most of the significant heat contribution in winter comes from sunlight entering south-facing windows. If possible, do not plant trees directly in front of south windows, and try not to site the house where existing trees will block this sunlight. Even bare deciduous trees can block 20 to 50 percent of winter sunlight, and this is particularly critical if their shadows fall across windows at midday.

The other heating strategy is to plant windbreaks, originally used as "shelterbelts" in the wide-open prairies of the Midwest and Plains states. Planting evergreen trees and shrubs to the north and west of a home saves energy on heating bills by forcing cold winds up and over the house and trapping the warmer air that escapes from buildings and soils. Once the evergreens are twice as tall as the building they are sheltering, the trees can reduce windspeeds there by as much as 85 percent.

For successful windbreaks, plant the trees close enough together that they create a dense screen, but not so close that the lower branches die from competition. Losing the lower branches allows cold air to blow in underneath the trees, spoiling the pocket of warmer air downwind. Evergreen shrubs set as foundation plantings on the north and west sides of a home or business can further insulate against heat loss.

Air Pollution Mitigation

Because the burning of fuels and forests has greatly increased, the amount of carbon dioxide in the atmosphere has risen dramatically over the last 200 years. Carbon in the atmosphere is a major cause of smog formation, heat-island effect, and respiratory problems. It traps heat and particulate pollution, causing human discomfort and illness and adding to the need for air conditioning. Increased air conditioner use strains utilities and increases the amount of fossil fuel they must burn, which in turn releases more heat and carbon into the atmosphere.

Trees mitigate air pollution by trapping and storing carbon. A mature tree absorbs more than 25 pounds of carbon per year from the atmosphere, storing it as wood and leafy material, and releases an average of 13 pounds of oxygen in the process (see Figure 2.4). One mature tree produces enough oxygen annually to satisfy the needs of a family of four for an entire year.

Trees also trap particulate pollution—airborne dust and chemical matter, removing it from the atmosphere and storing it on their leaves and stems until rain washes it to the ground. They are especially effective at capturing the airborne, smog-producing, and carcinogenic particles produced by fuel combustion and other such processes. A study of tree-planting efforts for the 1984 Summer

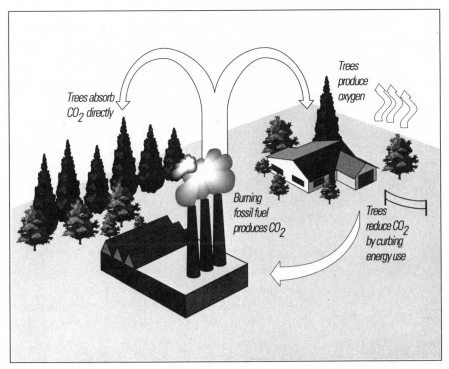

2.4 Trees mitigate air pollution by directly absorbing carbon dioxide (CO_2) from the atmosphere during photosynthesis. Cooling shade from trees also decreases air-conditioning use, which reduces the amount of CO_2 emitted by power plants.

Source: U.S. Environmental Protection Agency and AMERICAN FORESTS.

Olympics in Los Angeles estimated that 1 million new trees would remove 200 tons of particulate pollution per day once they were 10 years old.

The United States accounts for 25 percent of the world's total energy consumption and is thus responsible for much of the atmospheric carbon and particulate pollution in the global airstream. The Clinton administration's Climate Change Action Plan of 1993 identified tree planting as one of 50 voluntary actions aimed at reducing greenhouse gases to 1990 levels by the year 2000.

Developers and homeowners are in a unique position to contribute to the reduction of air pollution. By preserving some existing trees and planting new ones in their developments, they will provide healthier communities that help reduce pollution, lower atmospheric carbon, and slow warming trends.

Erosion Control and Water Quality

Trees, shrubs, and other vegetation intercept rainwater before it strikes the ground, absorbing some of the water, deflecting raindrops, and lessening their impact on the soils beneath. These processes reduce soil erosion. Roots also help hold the soil in place, further reducing the potential for runoff. Trees can absorb prodigious amounts of stormwater runoff; through evapotranspiration, a single large tree can process up to 400 gallons of water into the atmosphere per day, and this does not include water the tree retains for growth processes. Even desert trees serve as capable interceptors of stormwater runoff.

Forested land is the most effective at intercepting large amounts of rainwater and curtailing erosion and runoff. The water that runs off forested lands in heavy rains is also dramatically cleaner than runoff from disturbed or unvegetated land.

A Maryland Forest Service study of the Gunpowder Falls Basin in the Chesapeake Bay area found that, of the sediment deposited in the watershed yearly, forested land contributed some 50 tons for each square mile of forest. Compare that to 50 to 100 tons of sediment produced by each square mile of urban/suburban land (post-construction) in the region, 1,000 to 5,000 tons per square mile of farmland, and 25,000 to 50,000 tons per square mile of land under construction. Other studies have reached similar conclusions.

Trees and other vegetation have a vital role to play in protecting our soils, replenishing soil moisture and groundwater, and filtering rainfall, snowmelt, and stormwater runoff. Conversely, highway construction and land development can produce the most erosion and water degradation in a short period of time by disturbing vegetation and soils.

The federal Clean Water Act and, in many areas, local regulations require developers to protect water quality and to minimize soil erosion. Silt fences can trap some sediment in runoff but lack the ability trees and plants have to absorb and direct water underground. By conserving existing trees and underlying vegetation—especially by leaving more strategically located land undisturbed—developers can lessen runoff and comply with Clean Water Act stormwater requirements without relying so heavily on expensive stormwater retention facilities and sediment traps.

Psychological and Physical Health

When people are asked what trees do for their hometown, they most often mention their beauty, despite increasing data on energy savings and other quantifiable benefits. AMERICAN FORESTS commissioned an independent study of the environmental knowledge and attitudes of 1,200 households in six U.S. cities. Eighty-six percent of the respondents rated the beautification aspects of trees as "very important," with ratings of four or five on a five-point scale. Eighty-three percent gave high marks to trees' shade contributions, and 74 percent cited the wildlife habitat they provide. Significantly, 70 percent of respondents believed that trees "make you feel good."

Trees have a powerful bearing on our psychological well-being, one that we now know crosses over and affects our physical well-being, too. Developers who understand this psychological connection discover benefits that, though subconsciously communicated, can make a difference when it's time to sell their homes to customers.

The Stress Connection

Over the course of human history, the connection between people and trees has been strong. For primitive peoples, trees offered protection from violent storms and a safe haven from large predators.

Even in the modern world, people form deep subconscious connections with trees.

Virginia Tech's Bruce Hull compiled the reactions of survivors of Hurricane Hugo (1989) in Charleston, South Carolina. Although the storm devastated trees, homes, churches, and businesses with equal fury, the trees were considered the single greatest loss to the community by the largest number of respondents. Residents of Miami, Florida, and Mobile, Alabama, expressed similar sentiments over extensive tree loss in their communities following Hurricanes Andrew (1992) and Frederic (1979), respectively. Trees apparently provide much of what is unique and attractive in a community; they offer us a sense of place, a sense of stability.

According to some researchers, large, spreading trees seem to trigger a subconscious "calming" reaction even among urban dwellers. Research by Texas A&M's Roger Ulrich and others has shown that most people relax mentally and physically when surrounded by gardens or parks. But the understanding that trees release us from the stresses of urban living is hardly new. A century ago, Frederick Law Olmsted, designer of some of America's most famous and beautiful city parks, voiced his firm belief that the masses needed a place to escape the stresses of everyday modern living. New York City residents apparently shared his views, for during Olmsted's work on Central Park, nearby property values increased ninefold, compared with a twofold increase for the rest of the city.

Sound Effects

Not all of the stress relief provided by trees is ephemeral. Some of that peace comes from a very real physical benefit—noise buffering.

Trees help intercept noise. According to the U.S. Department of Transportation, they are not as effective as large, constructed sound barriers, but they do block noise, especially when planted in contiguous rows grown to widths of 16 feet or more. Trees also visually soften constructed barriers and offer residents a visual suggestion that noise is being blocked. If, because of a row of trees, a highway is not plainly visible from a house, residents don't consciously "listen" for highway sounds.

Trees dull or soften sound waves that attempt to pass through them and further dampen these sounds by adding noises of their own, a phenomenon called "masking." The sound of rustling leaves is, according to Illinois researchers Herbert Schroeder and Charles Lewis, similar to "white noise," which researchers have demonstrated is effective in relaxing people.

Getting Well, Staying Well

Many of the researchers who have studied trees' psychological benefits point to physical data to verify how strongly our psychological state affects our physical one. That data also proves how strongly our surroundings affect us; trees can have a great deal to do not only with whether we stay happy or relaxed but whether we stay well.

Daily stresses and anxieties take a toll on the human mind and can suppress the immune system. Findings gathered by researchers Hull and Ulrich suggest that nature in general and trees in particular offer restoration to the human mind and body through passive viewing. This allows the immune system to power up again to a more normal protective capacity. Other research has found that individuals who viewed nature scenes with trees had lower blood pressure levels than individuals who viewed urban scenes without trees.

Just how far restoration can go was echoed in one of Ulrich's most widely publicized projects, a nine-year study of gallbladder surgery patients at a Pennsylvania hospital. All candidates selected were similar in age and condition and had the same surgical procedure performed. Patients whose rooms looked out on a pleasant scene with trees required fewer painkillers and had 10 percent shorter hospital stays than the patients whose windows faced a brick wall.

Passive viewing of trees and nature seems to meet a fundamental human need. While the restorative therapy takes place largely on hidden levels within the mind and body, many people are conscious of the good feelings that trees bring them. A developer who understands the powerful subconscious magic of trees will create a higher-quality product that inherently appeals to more home buyers.

Back to Nature

Not all home buyers limit themselves to passive viewing of trees and nature, however. For a hefty share of the market, a well-treed, well-planned development can offer even more benefits. According to the U.S. Fish and Wildlife Service, half of American adults participate in some form of outdoor recreation involving nature. Since urbanization and reduced leisure time have made rural areas less of a recreational option, people increasingly seek the outdoors on their decks, in backyard gardens, and at local parks. As a result, trees and natural environments close to home are becoming a greater priority for more and more home buyers.

To meet the growing recreational and environmental needs of both people and wildlife, many communities are encouraging the creation of greenways and natural woodland backyards (see Figure 2.5). Greenways are basically linear strips of land that provide contiguous belts of trees for recreation and wildlife.

2.5 People increasingly seek natural areas and trails close to home.

Source: United Parcel Service headquarters, Atlanta, Georgia. Reprinted with permission from Arborguard Tree Specialists.

Greenways offer joggers, cyclists, and pedestrians a place free of traffic. By providing contiguous cover and making it possible for birds and animals to avoid vehicular traffic as well, greenways make better sanctuaries for wildlife than isolated parcels. Greenways' benefits are enhanced when they are preserved or built along waterways; this puts the lush vegetation to work filtering and intercepting runoff.

Native or naturalized yards are another item many look for when selecting a home—especially in areas with few or no nearby parks or greenways. Yards containing preserved or transplanted trees and native understory plants require less maintenance and—so long as they are native or well adapted—handle extreme weather better than most grasses. They are also more attractive to birds and wildlife, which many homeowners find appealing.

Homeowners today want services that cater to their leisure interests. American Lives Inc., a San Francisco-based firm that interviews approximately 100,000 consumers a year for the real estate industry, recently found that homeowners increasingly value natural areas, walking or bicycle trails, and small parks over more traditional amenities such as golf courses and tennis courts.[1] Other surveys have found that lots near parks and other open space sell better and appreciate in value faster over time. Developers can use cluster development, an innovative site-planning technique, to accommodate these recreational amenities (see Chapter 4).

Advantages for Developers and Builders

If trees provided no other benefit than oxygen, they would still be worth preserving. But trees offer financial benefits to people and communities—and some specific benefits for developers.

Enhancing Property Values and Sales

According to 1,350 real estate agents surveyed by Bank America Mortgage, more than half believed that trees have a positive impact on potential buyers' impressions of homes and neighborhoods. A whopping 84 percent felt that a home with trees would be as much as 20 percent more salable than a home without trees.

2.6 A new development with mature trees has greater appeal to home buyers and is thus more marketable.

Source: Photograph of Deerfield Knoll, Media, Pennsylvania, by Debra L. Bassert, NAHB.

Participants discussed properties ranging in price from $60,000 to $300,000. Fifty-six percent of real estate agents surveyed felt that healthy shade trees are a strong factor in a home's salability; 60 percent thought that healthy shade trees have a big effect on a potential buyer's first impression; and 62 percent said the presence of healthy shade trees strongly affects a potential buyer's impression of a block or neighborhood (see Figure 2.6).

Indiana's C.P. Morgan, Virginia's Hank Meyer and Clem Carlisle, and Oklahoma's David Yost are known for taking extra measures to plan and provide for trees. They consider such steps worthwhile because homes in their developments consistently sell for more money and at faster rates than the market average for their areas.

Meyer and Carlisle's Woodlake development in Chesterfield County, Virginia, has enjoyed a 40 percent market share in its price ranges. Fully half of those purchasing homes in Woodlake come from other parts of the country, attracted by the environmental quality of the development.

C.P. Morgan has found that his wooded lots sell for an average of 20 percent more than similarly sized nonwooded lots. A few nice trees can add $10,000 to $15,000 to a base lot price of $60,000. And a Pennsylvania development firm, Realen Homes, has found that mature trees in new developments help those communities compete more effectively against older, established neighborhoods. Faster lot absorption and sales mean reduced debt load and risk for the developer and less money spent on advertising. This increases project success and frees valuable funds for use in other projects.

Many people mistakenly believe that tree preservation and tree planting are fiscally feasible only on upscale, expensive properties. Yet Oklahoma City developer Yost saw a difference of more than 20 percent even in the prices of his Apple Valley subdivision lots, which were in the modest $23,000 range. Studies in some regions of the country have found trees make a difference of as much as 30 percent in the selling price of lots.

Smaller lots and parcels often pose a greater environmental challenge. Some of the best success stories involving these smaller sites have begun to emerge through Global ReLeaf for New Communities. Preserving trees on a hilly, heavily wooded, 12-acre parcel required innovative financing and construction techniques for Indiana developer Brad Chambers of The Buckingham Companies. Chambers' plans called for building a 130-unit apartment complex in Bloomington, Indiana, that followed the federal Low-Income Housing Tax Credit program guidelines. A development similar in size and design stood on adjacent land.

The site's lush vegetation, however, inspired Chambers to rethink his design. Roads and parking areas were downsized and relocated to save trees, and redesigned units were fit into hillsides rather than built on slabs. These efforts reduced the need for grading.

The changes were not cheap. Retaining walls and root-saving tree wells drove project costs some $300,000 over those for a traditional, similarly sized project. This translated to $2.50 in additional costs per square foot of construction. When the development was finished, however, the results were astonishing for a project that includes low-income units. Buffer strips of preserved native trees offered privacy between buildings and improved the aesthetics of the development. A stormwater retention pond, carved from an existing ravine and planted with native trees and shrubs, offered wildlife habitat and created a recreational amenity. Dozens of native and exotic trees were added elsewhere on the site.

Chambers can list many tangible benefits The Buckingham Companies reaped from Bradford Ridge Apartments. The 130-unit complex reached full occupancy within its first year, requiring minimal advertising. Chambers noted greater retention than the norm for resident occupancy, which can save thousands of dollars on apartment remodeling costs. Bradford Ridge increased sales traffic in the broader community and enhanced its image as well.

Thanks to the site's outstanding natural beauty, the company was able to charge more for units with views, increasing total annual income by about $11,000. The overall value of the property also increased. The increased income allowed the developer to secure an additional mortgage, which helped offset the added costs of the tree-saving measures.

Such benefits are even sweeter in tough times and in tough markets. During the recession of 1991-92, extensive tree-saving efforts by Massachusetts developer James Brady qualified his seniors' housing project, The Maples at Wenham, for the Global ReLeaf New Community designation—and its sales stayed ahead of the competition in a very soft New England market.

Saving Costs

Michael T. Rose was one of the first developers to commit wholeheartedly to tree conservation measures as a way of doing business. As one whose company has added $2.2 billion to Maryland and Virginia's tax base since 1975, he is also mindful of the bottom line. Rose's perspective is that, while it costs money to save trees, it also costs money to chop them down. He finds that tree conservation is usually a trade-off, with savings on some items and greater costs on others. He also acknowledges that "no builder wants to spend money to get less money" and considers it a fact that home buyers will pay more for homes with trees.

Saving trees means avoiding grading within the trees' root zones. And when developers do not have to grade land or clear and grub trees, it means they save money. Less money must also then be spent on landscaping, or the same landscaping budget can be used to accomplish greater results—planting more trees to augment the mature trees left on-site.

Because trees serve such a multitude of environmental purposes, they can often both reduce the need for costly infrastructure, such as engineered stormwater systems, and enhance a site. By leaving a buffer of native trees around the stormwater pond he built for Bradford Ridge, developer Chambers did more than contribute to the purity of his site's stormwater and reduce its flow. He created a wildlife habitat and recreational area that further increased the property's value.

Mature trees that are preserved during development add more value to a lot than post-construction landscaping. A more established look can help a home or subdivision better compete with existing homes in older neighborhoods. As Linda Hales wrote in the *Washington Post*—in reporting on NAHB's unveiling of "The New American Home '95"—building around a site's existing trees gives a home "instant history."[2] Most tree protection ordinances also grant landscaping credits when existing trees are protected.

The least expensive way to save trees is to save them in groups, for example, in common areas. Working with local regulators to obtain permission for clustered homes is a way to maintain the necessary density while preserving significant stands of trees.

Enhancing the Developer's and Builder's Image

Like any businessperson, developers and builders understand the value of community goodwill. Nearly all grapple from time to time with trying to improve the environmental image some people associate with land development and construction. Most know that a high approval rating is the best advertising around; it can't be bought at any price and can pave the way for faster, easier approvals down the road.

Over the last 25 years, America has become a much more complex place for developers and builders. Federal mandates such as the Clean Water Act hold them responsible for erosion control and for protecting wetlands; other mandates dictate floodplain and wildlife protection. Local zoning and subdivision requirements have become complex and approvals lengthier and much less certain. Rising insurance costs, local politics, and no-growth sentiments further complicate land development. The public, too, is increasingly demanding in its expectations inside and outside a home. Trees and the creation of natural areas, such as greenways, offer a simple but effective means of enhancing the perceived quality of a home and, as a result, of benefiting a developer's image.

The Buckingham Companies' president Chambers received letters of commendation from local community leaders for his work in creating Bradford Ridge Apartments. Chambers has been assured that his efforts there will pay off handsomely in cooperation in the future.

Oklahoma City developer Yost was forging partnerships with diverse groups locally and statewide before and after receiving national Global ReLeaf New Community designation for his Apple Valley project. These efforts have included membership on a local tree commission, frequent speaking engagements, and serving as liaison between conservation concerns and the state's home builders association. As a result of his many efforts, Yost possesses an award few developers receive: Conservationist of the Year from Oklahoma's statewide chapter of the Soil and Water Conservation Society.

Maryland developer Rose has been doing environmentally conscious construction since the 1970s and has received regional and even national acclaim, including numerous awards, for his efforts. Rose used his track record and knowledge of trees and their benefits to negotiate significant regulatory concessions and save trees in his planned community of Northridge. These concessions allowed him to build a more desirable community with an authentic rural feel—and to save thousands of trees and protect more land and soil. His Solomon's Landing project in Solomons, Maryland, was even designated an Urban Wildlife Sanctuary by the National Institute for Urban Wildlife.

Owners of a pristine tract of land in Illinois worried about what would happen to the land after it left their hands. The fact that developer Roger Gatewood had received a Global ReLeaf New Community designation earned him added credibility and trust that gave him an edge in bidding on the property. In commenting on his company's tree conservation efforts and participation in Global ReLeaf for New Communities, Westfield Development Corporation president Gatewood said he had gained "a new and significant level of credibility with land sellers, municipalities, and the media."

Advantages for Communities

Trees offer not only broad benefits to humans and wildlife, but tangible benefits to homeowners, developers, and communities. When a developer builds successfully with trees, a circle of benefits begins to form.

Indiana developer Chambers fulfilled a market need for affordable housing when he built Bradford Ridge Apartments under the federal Low-Income Housing Tax Credit guidelines. By building with trees, though, he improved both environmental quality and project appeal. Other developers in the Bloomington area are now trying to emulate Chambers' higher standards. Just as the value of real estate surrounding Central Park soared after Olmsted's work there, property values at Bradford Ridge have been enhanced and will likely continue to climb over time.

Chambers also noted that Bradford Ridge's environmental quality has reduced the resident turnover rate. Residents' permanence usually has a positive effect on real estate values. Enhanced property values and aesthetic appeal also create an environment that is more marketable to business owners and improve a municipality's tax base (see Figure 2.7). Significantly, trees offer communities another benefit: They increase in value with minimal maintenance throughout their existence.

2.7 Trees help create a sense of community.

Source: Photograph by Debra L. Bassert, NAHB.

Conclusion

Trees offer developers and communities a full spectrum of benefits. But developers who wish to offer healthy, viable, and valuable trees on their project sites must plan for them as intensively as they plan for the buildings, roads, and utilities. Successful integration of trees and development is not an "either/or" proposition. It means seeing protection and damage prevention as an equal part of the development package. The rest of this book will explain how to achieve this result.

Developers and builders who build this way reap their own benefits from trees. Their efforts produce a product that is better for home buyers, the environment, and the community. In the process, they garner enhanced business success and a better image for themselves and land development as a profession.

---

1. © 1995, Washington Post Writers Group. Reprinted with permission.
2. © 1995 *The Washington Post.* Reprinted with permission.

Chapter 3

How a Tree Works

The survival or death of trees on construction sites is attributable neither to green thumb magic nor to capriciousness on the part of trees. Some species are more difficult to work around than others, but the loss of a tree can almost always be both understood and avoided. This chapter will explain some of the basics of tree growth and survival, as well as how trees are affected by various construction practices common on development sites (see Figure 3.1).

Tree Physiology

The Roots

Woody trees are anchored by between 4 and 11 large underground limbs known as roots. Woody trees develop both major, or transport, roots and absorption roots, the smaller feeder roots that extend from the major ones. Major roots begin growing when the tree is a small seedling and transport fluids and nutrients as well as anchor the tree. The major roots also receive all-important carbohydrates, manufactured by the tree's leaves and then made available to the entire root system. If a major root is removed or killed, a tree generally cannot add another one; it must try to survive with the remaining large roots. This is especially true of older trees.

The absorption roots are small but form vast networks that fan out from the ends of the major roots. They range from the thickness of a human hair to that of pencil lead. Absorption roots gather two vital products: water and mineral nutrients. The need for water is

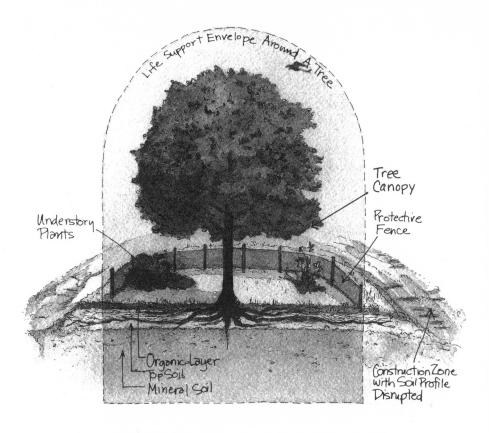

Life Support Envelope Around A Tree

Tree Canopy

Protective Fence

Understory Plants

Organic Layer
Top Soil
Mineral Soil

Construction Zone
with Soil Profile
Disrupted

3.1 Most tree roots grow in the top 18 inches of soil and extend well beyond the tree canopy. Establish a tree protection zone—a life support envelope for the tree inside which no construction activity should occur—to minimize root disturbance.

Source: Reprinted with permission from Bono Mitchell Graphics.

obvious; trees use minerals as essential supplements that help build wood and leaves or as a source of necessary chemicals. Absorption roots are much like human hair in that a small percentage die every day and are replaced. Stresses such as droughts and hard freezes kill them in large numbers. And trees shed these roots in bulk—replacing them anew every winter.

A tree's major roots begin as a pronounced flare at the base of the trunk, above the soil line. Progressing downward and out from the trunk flare, the major roots snake underground at various levels. These levels have much to do with the depth and porosity of the soil: The deeper, more lightweight, and well-aerated the soil, the deeper the tree's roots tend to travel. Regardless, 85 percent of a tree's major roots are concentrated in the top 18 inches of soil—99 percent are above the 3-foot level.

As major roots give way to absorption roots, the roots become shallower still. Absorption roots grow mostly upward, reaching for water and nutrients that fall to the ground. They concentrate in the loose, nutrient-rich top few inches of soil known as the "duff layer"—a feature not usually present in urban soils that have been disturbed.

Another reason the absorption roots concentrate in the topmost layer of soil is that they require oxygen to use food effectively. Tree roots must breathe—they won't grow in airless or poorly oxygenated soils. This is important for developers to realize, as it means limiting the amount of paving and soil compaction around trees earmarked for protection.

How far do tree roots travel from the trunk of a tree? Most people think of trees as being shaped like an upended dumbbell, with the root area and crown roughly equal in shape as well as size. Research has shown that a tree actually more closely resembles a wineglass set on a dinner plate. The base of the wineglass would be the part of the trunk where the major roots flare outward. The dinner plate would be the rest of the root system, extending far beyond the "dripline," the edge of the tree's canopy. Tree roots extend an average distance of $1\frac{1}{2}$ times the canopy diameter and can extend up to 5 times that diameter. Efforts to preserve trees should encompass at least as much root space as is contained under a tree's dripline.

In real-life situations, the wineglass would not always be centered on the plate. In other words, tree roots are not perfectly symmetrical around the tree. When a tree is in a dry climate, on a steep slope, or bordered on one or more sides by compacted soil, the roots often will reach farther in the direction of needed water or oxygen—usually downslope.

Drawing a tree onto a blueprint and indicating a perfect circle around it for a protection zone is rarely sufficient planning to protect special trees. Planning to save a mature tree, and especially a large one, means calling in a certified arborist or other natural resource expert to verify the actual location of the tree's roots and how far they extend. The actual cost of saving a tree's roots may be no greater than the cost of preserving that perfect circle. But verifying the actual location of tree roots promises much better results.

Roots will grow anywhere if given a suitable environment. Ensuring that suitable environment, however, means providing permeable soil (to a depth of at least 18 inches) that does not remain waterlogged after rains and that is not too acidic or alkaline (usually close to neutral in its pH level). Also, the soil should have a porosity of 50 percent for optimum root growth; many post-construction soils are compacted to a mere 10 percent porosity, which will kill trees. Since absorption roots are concentrated near the ends of major roots, fertilizing is most effective when done near a tree's dripline and beyond, rather than close to the trunk.

Some tree species have developed roots with special ways of surviving in dense, airless soil, among them baldcypress, black gum, alder, ash, poplar, willow, and tupelo. These trees have been a boon to urban areas, which provide the minimal requirements for their survival.

However, most trees cannot survive long-term in soil conditions created by conventional construction methods. Besides suffering from compaction, soils in construction areas lose beneficial organisms when they are disturbed. These beneficial organisms, including certain mycorrhizal fungi, help trees by aerating soils and making certain nutrients more readily available to absorption roots. To keep a tree healthy—and to assure good results with added landscaping—the root zones should be avoided altogether. If root zones have to be disturbed, soils should be amended with composts or nutrients after construction, then mulched. This helps return the soil to a more natural, forest-like environment.

Phloem, Xylem, and Cambium

Few people realize that most of the wood in a living, healthy tree is already dead. The living wood lies just beneath the bark, but the central wood in a large tree is all dead, solidified and retained for support purposes only (except in palms, where these functions are reversed).

If not for the weight of seeds and fruit and the abuses of wind and weather, all trees could function as hollow entities, without the central wood. When a tree is sheltered from strong winds, it may survive, grow, and bear fruit for many years despite "heart rot"—pathogens that break through the tree's natural defense system to decay dead wood tissue in its center.

Just beneath a tree's bark are three relatively shallow layers of living tissue that support the crown mass above and connect it with the roots: phloem ("FLOW-um"), xylem ("ZY-lum"), and cambium ("KAM-bee-um"). The phloem layer is located directly beneath a tree's bark. It transports food manufactured by the leaves—carbohydrates (sugars)—to all portions of the tree as needed. Phloem cells not only transport food downward from the canopy, but occasionally upward as well, particularly when a tree begins to grow in springtime.

The xylem cells transport water and minerals up and down the tree. As a tree grows, the older, inner xylem cells "clog" with fibers and a product known as lignin. Arranged like interlocking bricks, these solidified cells die and compose the heartwood—the sturdy supportive wood in the center of the tree. As the cells die, they become much larger than they were when formed. The result: 70 to 90 percent (by bulk) of a tree's wood is dead, although this dead wood contains only about 20 percent of the tree's total number of wood cells.

The layer of cells between the phloem and the xylem is the cambium layer. Its outer portion generates new phloem cells and its inner portion, new xylem cells. The cambium also manufactures special defensive cells known as parenchyma cells.

When a tree dies from injury, the wound may not appear serious enough to cause death. But a tree—big and tough as it may seem—simply does not have the vast, living reserves its size would suggest. A clear cycle of decline can be set in motion by injury or stress. This mortality spiral is examined later in this chapter.

Bark: The Tree's Skin

For trees, bark functions much like skin does for humans. It protects the more delicate tissues underneath from infections, predators, and becoming dried out. Like human skin, bark is composed of nonliving tissue on the outside and living tissue on the inside.

Some barks are thick and corky—too dry and unpleasant for most insects to chew through. In dry climates, many trees produce thick bark to help conserve water and protect against the heat of frequent fires. California's famed coast live oaks share this adaptation, along with many pines. Other barks are thin but may be loaded with heavy waxes or offensive chemicals that are toxic to pests.

Since the bark is a tree's first line of defense, keeping it free from damage is essential to tree protection. When a tree's bark is scraped or knocked off, the tree is vulnerable to infection and pests. A bark wound does not "heal" but is walled off by a tree over time; new bark and tissue form around the edges of the wound, enclosing it. This makes the case for keeping away heavy equipment, animals, vandals, and careless people during construction (see Chapter 4). Even the time-honored practice of carving initials into a tree trunk may be all the invitation a lethal fungus or insect pest needs.

Sealed Fate

When a tree's bark is wounded, fungi or bacteria usually invade. The tree's special parenchyma cells then act to seal off the wound and keep these invaders from overrunning the entire plant. Parenchyma cells have a role similar to that of humans' white blood cells. They carry infection-fighting compounds, releasing them at the site of the wound. They can also cause other cells to wall off wounds and infection and keep them from spreading.

A tree always maintains a certain number of parenchyma cells scattered throughout its tissues and steps up their production when wounded or threatened by infection or insect pests. This requires additional energy, however, and so all the tree's other processes—such as photosynthesis, respiration, and tissue growth—are cut back.

Trees concentrate some of their parenchyma cells in "branch collars"—the flared areas where branches attach to a tree's trunk. When pruning, therefore, cut the limbs off where they attach to the branch collar (see Figure 3.2); never cut limbs off flush to the trunk. Cutting off a tree's branch collar removes the extra parenchyma cells that hasten the sealing off of such a wound, making it harder and slower for the tree to do this. It also leaves fewer parenchyma cells on hand to fight off any opportunistic infections that might arise.

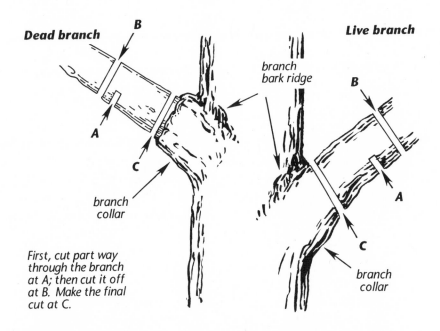

Dead branch

Live branch

branch
bark ridge

branch
collar

First, cut part way
through the branch
at A; then cut it off
at B. Make the final
cut at C.

branch
collar

3.2 A correct pruning technique uses a three-cut method of removing a branch to avoid tearing bark and retains the branch collar to hasten the tree's ability to seal cuts.

Source: Drawing is copyrighted by, and reproduced with the permission of, the Minnesota Extension Service, University of Minnesota, from its publication FO-6135, *Protecting Trees from Construction Damage* (revised 1995).

Watch That Mulch!

As a soil protector, mulch plays an important role in nurturing trees. But it can have just the opposite effect if allowed to touch the trunk of a tree. Since it holds moisture, mulch often contains fungi, and many fungi are lethal to trees—particularly if they penetrate a tree's bark. The tree's trunk flare must remain uncovered (except in palm trees). Trees that have mulch piled against their trunks usually respond in one of two ways. If possible, they alter the trunk flare so that it becomes part of the root, sending new roots from the flare out into the mulch. Unlike soil-bound roots, these suffer extremes of heat and cold, and as the mulch decomposes and shrinks, they may be exposed and eventually die.

Alternatively, trees go into a slow decline, attacked and weakened by fungi at their base. Many will weaken with few visible symptoms, then—perhaps after years of incorrect mulching—die suddenly at the first severe drought, flood, or hard freeze.

Chlorophyll, Inc.

Plants are unique in their ability to capture pure energy—in the form of sunlight—and convert it to forms of energy (sugars and carbohydrates) that living creatures can use. This manufacturing process not only provides essential oxygen to animals and humans but also a vital balance to the earth's climate.

How do trees manufacture this "bio-energy"? Chlorophyll—the green matter trees produce in their leaves and stems—intercepts, captures, and stores incoming solar energy as carbohydrates, mostly as sugars. Whenever the tree requires energy, it breaks some of these bonds and accesses the stored energy through a process called respiration. Oxygen, a principal by-product of this process, is released in water vapor.

As leaves and stems convert sunlight into food for all portions of the tree, underground feeder roots are absorbing necessary minerals and water from the soil. Major (transport) roots pull energy from the tree's crown and burn it as fuel, sending life-giving water and minerals to the trunk in return. At the trunk, a thin band of phloem tissue stores and disperses energy-rich carbohydrates, while xylem tissue receives water and minerals from the roots. The xylem layer stores some of this and disperses the rest as needed.

Stripping a tree's leaves during the growing season is the equivalent of removing solar panels from a solar-powered home. Similarly, wounding a tree branch directly threatens the leaves on that branch and indirectly threatens to weaken the rest of the tree. While pruning is a good horticultural practice in the hands of an arborist, it can weaken a tree by removing leaves and limbs needed for energy production.

When leaves die during the growing season, if it's not due to drought, it's usually because of a severe attack by pests or disease or because a tree's roots, trunk, or limbs have been badly damaged.

Tree Life Cycles

As explained in Chapter 2, older, more mature trees tend to bring the most value to a property. The reasons are simple: Mature trees produce more oxygen, have greater summer cooling and winter heat-retention capabilities, and usually offer the strongest psychological and aesthetic benefits. However, mature trees usually don't tolerate stress—including the effects of construction—as well as younger trees do. Sometimes this is readily apparent: Young trees may bend easily and survive storms that shatter or uproot stiffer, older trees.

But young trees also have a high percentage of leaf mass (the energy-generating portion) compared with woody mass (the portion that requires energy to maintain and defend). They are more resilient to change and certain stresses because they have relatively little tissue that requires maintenance and can keep a high percentage of energy stored in their living tissues. This, coupled with the fact that young trees still have much growing to do, gives them greater ability to adapt to changes in their environment.

As a tree grows larger, it can store less of its energy for stressful times. The amount of existing tissue is so great that the tree must operate near its full, healthy capacity just to maintain the status quo. Nearly all the energy a large tree can produce is taken up by keeping existing tissue alive, defending itself, and producing pollen and seeds.

Physical Injuries and Pathogens

Since mature trees are not growing and expanding their tissue space very much, it's easy to understand why they are particularly vulnerable to physical injury or pathogens. Any wood killed by disease or injury is walled off, unable to pass sugars, water, minerals, or parenchyma cells. Once these damaged or infected areas are sealed off, the tree routes necessary elements around them for the rest of its life. A devastating injury or series of small injuries can produce so much dead, or "clogged," wood that the tree can no longer transport sufficient water and nutrients where they're needed. This chokes the tree in much the same way that human arteries can clog and eventually cut off vital blood supplies.

Death by Stress

A developer may opt to preserve a large, dominating tree on a site, only to see it die a few years later. When neither the trunk nor the limbs show signs of physical injury, this loss can be particularly exasperating. This sort of death often gives the illusion that trees are capricious—that they just "decide" to die. In fact, any stress on a mature tree causes it to deplete its energy reserves. If the stress continues after the reserves are depleted, the tree is forced to die back, and fatal decline often follows.

When wounds force a tree to step up the production and use of parenchyma cells, growth and routine maintenance suffer. For example, if a truck runs over a large tree's roots, one or more of the tree's major roots may be broken and tens of thousands of absorption roots crushed or choked off by compacted soil. But the crown demands the same amount of water and nutrients formerly supplied by the full set of roots. With some of those roots out of action, the tree can no longer maintain all its leaves, so photosynthesis declines. A reduction in photosynthesis means less energy available to grow new roots or replace the leaves that have declined, forcing the tree to slow down even more. Branches begin to die back, further reducing the available leaf space for photosynthesis. Production and maintenance of phloem and xylem cells are cut back, reducing growth. New roots have a tough time forming in the compacted soil.

Arborists call the vicious circle this sets in motion a "mortality spiral." One condition aggravates the other, leaving the tree an easy target for insects and disease. Droughts, floods, fires, freezes, and other common environmental stresses can hasten this process. With little energy left to fight off invaders or infection, the tree is doomed (see Figure 3.3).

Sensitive Species

Some species of trees are more sensitive to construction activities than others and have a particularly hard time surviving root disturbance, including soil compaction, as well as actual physical injuries to roots. These species include beech, dogwood, sassafras, tupelo, white oak, northern pin oak, black oak, cherry, and most nut trees, such as black walnut, butternut, hickory, and pecan.

Green ash trees have difficulty recovering from wounds at the base of the trunk. For northern red oaks, the slightest wound to roots or trunk provides an easy entrance for oak wilt, a fatal disease common in much of the red oak's natural range. The same holds true for live oaks in Texas. Most oak wilts are primarily or partially

3.3 How a Tree Works

Follow the Roots

- ◆ Eighty-five percent of a tree's roots are in the top 18 inches of soil.
- ◆ Ninety-nine percent are in the top 3 feet of soil.
- ◆ Roots extend $1\frac{1}{2}$ to 5 times the diameter of a tree's canopy.

Trees Do Not Heal

- ◆ Living tissue lies just under the bark in a thin layer.
- ◆ Tissue seals wounds off.
- ◆ Damaged tissue is never repaired.

Timing is Everything

In temperate climates:

- ◆ In winter, trees are dormant above ground, and roots grow the most.
- ◆ In late spring and summer, trees actively grow above ground, and little root growth occurs below ground.

Tree Roots Need to Breathe, Too

- ◆ Grade changes of even a few inches will have adverse effects.
- ◆ Compaction will reduce the amount of space between soil particles, reducing available oxygen needed by roots.

---

soil borne—another reason why equipment and shoes should be kept out of root zones.

Pine trees are particularly susceptible to a different kind of problem that can arise after a site has been cleared: windthrow. Pines grown in clusters often have trunks that are too tall and narrow to support their crowns if they are deprived of the buffering their companions provide. As a result, newly isolated pines may snap in half during windstorms, and they are vulnerable to windthrow for at least 5 to 10 years. As a rule, pines are thus best preserved in groupings. An exception is a specimen pine that has grown in the open for a long time. These trees have thicker trunks and well-balanced crowns and have already held their own in the strong winds that batter isolated trees.

Exotics

The Sunbelt is experiencing a development boom that will likely continue, and one thing many newcomers want for their yards is warm-climate exotic trees they could only dream of before. From California, across southern New Mexico and Arizona, to the Gulf Coast, Florida, and the lower East Coast, tropical and subtropical plants are "hot."

Subtropical trees—such as camphors, live oaks, and certain eucalyptus—are really not so different from temperate-climate trees, but tropicals are a different story altogether. Unaccustomed to winter's chill, some tropicals rest and grow in brief spurts throughout the year. Some rest during the dry season, others according to their own cycles. Some seem literally not to rest at all.

As with temperate-climate trees, protected tropicals should have their root zones shielded from construction activities. Transplanted trees and ones added by landscapers after construction will recover best if the season is mild—neither severe heat nor cold—and rainfall is anticipated. In dry areas, such as California, watering will be critical; planting should wait, if possible, until the rainy season begins, unless ample water is available.

Palm trees are even more specialized; they are not true, woody trees and are very different structurally. Although most often thought of as growing in California and Florida, palms are hardly limited to those two states; several species can be grown across the Gulf Coast, some as far north as sheltered sections of Washington, DC. Their popularity with homeowners grows yearly, and nurseries are aggressively filling this demand.

A palm grows from its center, like a lily. Beneath the remnants of its leaf bases, the tough outer "wood" of its trunk (actually just bundled fibers) is dead—the exact reverse of a woody tree. Injuries to the outer "wood" will weaken a palm structurally, but they rarely cause the same degree of danger that surface wounds pose to a tree. However, damaging the new growth will kill that particular trunk. (Clustering palms, however, can sprout other crowns from the base of the plant.)

Palm roots can be as thin as a knitting needle and as thick as a finger; all look identical and all serve the same functions. A palm makes hundreds of these roots, radiating them out in all directions—sometimes 30 feet or more. Each serves as both transport root and feeder root, with the feeder root portion being a 2-inch absorbent area at the growing tip. If any roots are removed, root stubs left attached to the tree may help anchor it while it makes new roots, but because the absorbent tips are cut off, they cannot feed the tree. A palm recovers by generating new roots directly above the previous set. Since palms do all their growing during warm weather, a palm that will be dug, transplanted, or disturbed will recover best if it has an entire season of warm soil temperatures ahead of it. Contrary to the rules for planting a woody tree (outlined in Chapter 4), palms that are transplanted should be set deeper than they grew before. This way, new roots generated by the tree will not be exposed above ground and will instead go directly out into the soil.

How Construction Affects Trees

Before conserving trees on a construction site or leaving a site in suitable condition for planting new trees, developers, builders, and engineers need to realize how construction activities affect trees. Those who understand how trees function will have greater success saving, planting, and transplanting trees.

A tree's roots are perhaps its most critical part. Many trees with a healthy set of roots, left to recover in good, uncompacted soil, can fight insects and infections, grow new limbs, put on a new set of leaves, and flourish anew. Knowing that trees automatically replace large numbers of roots at predictable times each year will help developers as they prepare trees to withstand the stress of nearby construction or transplant trees ahead of time, allowing recovery time before construction begins (see Chapter 4).

In temperate climates, construction activities that affect tree roots are best done during fall and winter if possible. Although trees are nearly dormant above ground at this time, root growth, expansion, and healing is greatest, thus roots can recover better. In late spring and during the heat of summer, roots are providing water and nutrients for the greatest period of crown growth; however, little root growth takes place. Thus, during spring and summer, developers and builders will want to take extra care when working around trees. They may need to closely monitor the trees and provide additional water. In hot climates, where heat stress is a problem, avoid major root pruning during the hottest part of the summer.

Since trees don't have the means to "heal" wounds to their tissues, it is best to avoid injuring them in the first place. Trees must be kept free from construction-related injury and stress—from grading, compaction, contaminants, and wounds—as much as possible. To accomplish this, standard development practices that can damage trees should be examined in detail. Some damaging construction practices must be avoided near trees, while others need only be modified.

Grade Changes

Changing the grade near a tree affects the tree for several reasons:

◆ Tree roots are concentrated in the uppermost 18 to 36 inches of soil.

◆ Roots can grow considerable distances from the dripline of a tree's canopy and are not always contained in a perfect circle around the tree.

◆ Feeder roots in particular are concentrated in the top few richest inches of topsoil.

Grading around trees can have two serious negative effects. First, valuable nutrients in topsoil are removed. Second, the amount of ground moisture available to roots can decrease as vegetation is removed, soil is compacted by heavy equipment, and groundwater is redirected, leaving the soil relatively impervious to moisture.

The first negative effect is the more obvious. Grading destroys or removes the layers of soil most valuable to trees and plants. Stripping away soil layers means taking away all the roots, nutrients, earthworms, and beneficial fungi contained in those soils. Reducing a tree's root mass forces the tree to dip into its energy reserves. The tree may then lose some of its crown mass, which can stress the tree and invite pests and diseases. Damaged roots also create openings through which rot-causing agents can enter to destroy living tissues.

The second negative effect of grading is more long-term. Plants in the bulldozer's path typically are removed. These plants intercepted stormwater runoff, directing some of this water underground, and their roots kept the soil fractured and more permeable. This allowed subsurface water to rise more easily toward the surface and be available to tree roots.

Compaction from grading compounds the damage. The rock-hard soil is no longer hospitable to earthworms and other "tillers," and the roots of any remaining plants will find it difficult—if not impossible—to survive. By so drastically altering both the plants and the makeup of the soil itself, grading can lower the water table beyond the reach of tree roots. Grading that compacts soils can also cause subsurface water to detour around the affected area, cutting off trees' moisture. Further, grading can redirect runoff to other, un-graded areas—and to trees—that previously did not receive so much water, causing unhealthy new wet spots.

Rainfall typically runs off compacted soil rather than soaking in, increasing erosion, which then strips away more valuable topsoil and the few remaining nutrients. If moisture is able to penetrate compacted soil, the soil has great difficulty drying out since there is no airspace. Grading, therefore, almost always results in soils that are much drier or wetter than they were previously. For roots, this is the equivalent of being held underwater or set in cement. Few tree species can survive such treatment for long.

Fill That Kills

Adding fill during the grading process presents another set of problems for trees. Trucking or bulldozing in extra soil means heavy traffic that can crush roots and compact existing soils. More importantly, adding extra soil will almost always smother tree roots in the soils below.

When fill is added on top of grass or leaves, the plant matter often compacts into a thin, slimy layer that sheds water and prevents any air exchange. The fill layer also drastically reduces the amount of air that can reach the roots below. As little as an inch or two of additional soil can smother the roots of seedling trees; even large trees can die under just 4 or 5 inches of added fill. This is true even for soil that is scheduled for other uses and only temporarily stockpiled on a tree's roots.

The developer should call in a natural resource expert to determine the root zones of affected trees before any land is cut away. Retaining wall "islands" preserve these tree zones above the cuts. In filled areas, saving trees means constructing "tree wells" around them (see Figure 3.4). These are fairly expensive to install but are a tree's only hope in a fill situation (see Chapter 5 for more detail).

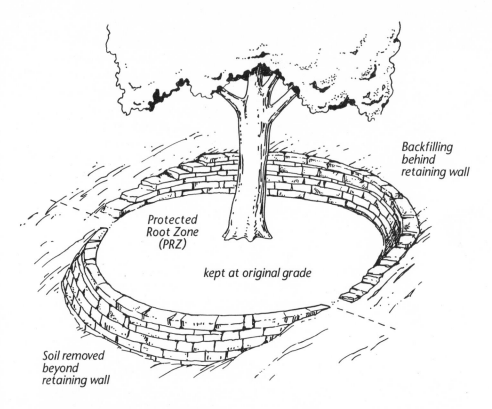

Backfilling
behind
retaining wall

Protected
Root Zone
(PRZ)

kept at original grade

Soil removed
beyond
retaining wall

**3.4 Retaining walls are used to protect a tree's root zone when natural grades must
be raised or lowered during construction.**

Source: Drawing is copyrighted by, and reproduced with the permission of, the Minnesota Extension Service,
University of Minnesota, from its publication FO-6135, *Protecting Trees from Construction Damage* (revised
1995).

Although the goal should be to minimize grading, some will be
necessary for roads and buildings to last. Ironically, developers
may need to seek exemption from costly and unnecessary grading
since local regulations often require more grading than is necessary. A well-presented plan can give developers a negotiating advantage with local regulators, showing them how reduced grading
can protect slopes and conserve trees without jeopardizing humans.

Incidental Soil Compaction

Land development often involves incidental soil compaction from
trucks and other heavy equipment within the construction site. And
it doesn't take a bulldozer, either. Any event that compresses soil

has the potential to harm trees and their environment. Vehicles, construction equipment, stored supplies, and even foot traffic all cause soil compaction (see Figure 3.5). Realen Homes, a development and building company in Pennsylvania, discovered that most soil compaction occurs with the first pass of a vehicle. This held true even for so-called lightweight pickup trucks. Tree roots do not distinguish between offending parties; when it comes to the end results, compaction is compaction. Examining the construction process in these terms opens the eyes to many potential causes of compaction damage.

Contaminants

Land development and construction use or involve many materials containing compounds that are potentially toxic to trees. Keep in mind that trees' large root systems can pick up contaminants from a considerable distance and that, once damaged, their tissues cannot heal.

3.5 Stockpiling construction materials within a tree's protected root zone, even for a short time, will compact soil and may cause root damage.

Source: Maryland Department of Natural Resources—Forest Service.

Trees thrive in a particular location not just because of climate but because they are well suited to the pH level (acidity or alkalinity) of local soils. Most trees prefer soils that are either neutral (balanced) or somewhat acidic. Leaf litter tends to be acidic, thus soils in heavily wooded areas tend to be on the acid side. Rich, organic soils also tend to be acid.

The weathering of concrete, brick, cement, plaster, and other building materials containing calcium are among the most common contaminants on development sites, at least in terms of injuring trees. The ingredients in concrete are strongly alkaline. When concrete mix is washed from trucks, tools, and equipment, for example, the level of acidity is drastically lowered in any soil it touches. This heightened alkalinity can reduce a tree's ability to absorb essential nutrients and also create an unfavorable environment for beneficial soil organisms. Many trees exposed to such a shock will die, though death may often take two years or more. Smaller native plants, especially rhododendrons and azaleas, also will die or be severely injured.

Before using concrete, carefully consider landscape plans and the surroundings. Over time, concrete slab foundations will leach lime into the soil, eventually raising the alkalinity nearby and possibly killing nearby dogwoods, azaleas, rhododendrons, and other acid-loving landscape plants. The deaths will be slow enough to cause many homeowners to try numerous and expensive remedies without ever understanding what is actually wrong.

Numerous other products used in development or construction can damage trees. Stains, paints, and paint thinners can easily spill and are hard to clean up. Oil-based products and those with ether/alcohol bases can kill roots, wood, and leaves on contact. Even latex paints can suffocate small plants or portions of larger ones by blocking sunlight from leaves and preventing respiration. Less harmful versions of many traditional construction products are now available and should be considered.

The asphalt and tar used in paving are oil-based products and are often lethal to tree roots just because of the temperatures they must be heated to. Cookers used to melt tar radiate heat and fumes that can kill roots and branches, so they should be kept at a distance from trees. Incidental contamination from other pollutants spilled by people or equipment can be just as damaging to trees. A well-known expert on protecting trees during construction once told of taking great measures to save a magnificent oak on a development site, only to have someone on lunch break kill the tree by changing a vehicle's oil in the tree's root zone. The only innovation that will protect trees from such products and procedures is the education and monitoring of all members of the development team, the builders, and the subcontractors. This is discussed in detail in Chapter 5.

Trenching

Chief among the development steps that result in the greatest destruction of natural resources are grading and utility installation. Trenching to install utilities involves digging from the surface down to a prescribed depth—usually 2 feet or more below the soil surface. Since the majority of tree roots are concentrated in the top 3 feet of soil, trenching within the root zone of a tree inevitably severs roots. The closer the pass to the tree trunk, the greater the percentage of roots lost. Since nearly all trees have at most 11 major roots—sometimes as few as 4—losing any of these can immediately render a tree worthless.

The damage is often magnified by trenching equipment—such as backhoes—that rip and crush roots, leaving large, traumatic wounds that are difficult to heal and offer gaping points of entry for disease. When a root must be cut, vibratory knives and surgically sharp rock cutters are better than backhoes. This is akin to a person having an arm removed with a clean, razor-sharp, surgical saw rather than ripped off. An even better option is to avoid root zones as much as possible and then to use tunneling devices instead of trenchers to penetrate root zones. Tunnels, dug 3 feet deep or deeper, usually have minimal impact on tree roots (see Figure 3.6).

Wounds to Trunks and Limbs

The last major threat trees face during development and construction is the wounding of their trunks, limbs, and canopies by people and heavy equipment (see Figure 3.7). A crane that swings too close to a tree or a truck that hits a trunk or limb can wreak havoc on even the most vigorous trees. Under the very best of circumstances, the wounded tree will carry a permanent, though eventually hidden, scar. At worst, pests or disease will kill a valuable tree and then use it as a base for attacking other trees and plants.

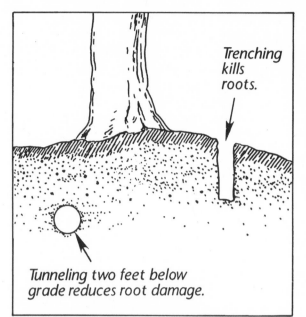

Trenching kills roots.

Tunneling two feet below grade reduces root damage.

3.6 Tunneling, when feasible, is preferable to trenching, as it disturbs far fewer roots.

Source: Drawing is copyrighted by, and reproduced with the permission of, the Minnesota Extension Service, University of Minnesota, from its publication FO-6135, *Protecting Trees from Construction Damage* (revised 1995).

3.7 Heavy equipment can damage tree limbs and trunks and should be kept out of the tree protection zone.

Source: Photograph by Gary Moll, AMERICAN FORESTS.

In the past, paints, bricks and mortar, and even tar products have been used on tree wounds in hopes of "healing" them or sealing them off from pests and disease. No evidence exists that these well-intentioned efforts do anything to help an injured tree. In fact, tar kills adjacent tissues, and water and rot-causing organisms can usually penetrate beneath it—hidden from view but destroying the tree. When physical wounds occur, it is best to either remove the tree or allow it to close off the wounds itself with its parenchyma cells. A professional arborist should examine the tree and make recommendations.

Conclusion

Because trees cannot heal as animals do, they require preventive care. If a tree is worth saving, it is worth having a root protection zone. Chapters 4 and 5 will discuss tree protection techniques and enforcement measures.

A natural resource expert offers a level of expertise that helps ensure tree health and survival. This specialist's role in the development process is discussed at the beginning of Chapter 4. Conserving trees during development is not so much difficult as different from methods in the past. Many innovative methods have been devised to conserve trees, and the extra efforts are paying for themselves. When coupled with an understanding of how trees work, these innovations greatly improve the builder's and developer's ability to build in harmony with the natural environment.

Chapter 4

Trees as Part of the Plan

B uilding with the environment means seeing planned development and natural systems as intricately linked and viewing
natural resources as an opportunity rather than a constraint. The developer or builder who fully integrates trees and other natural resources into all construction planning creates a setting in which
natural elements and development enhance one another.

Urban forestry research is shedding increasing light on how to
modify construction techniques to conserve more trees. What's
been learned along the way, however, is that it's not just altered
construction practices, but a different management approach that offers real success in blending trees and development. This approach
involves education, communication, and coordination among many
players: local officials, subcontractors, home builders, and home
buyers who purchase finished lots.

Developing a site while making the best use of trees and natural resources also requires professional expertise. This chapter details the urban forestry specialist's contributions to the development
team and describes the recommended development process.

The Development Team

At the very outset of a project, the developer needs to assemble a
team of planning professionals. The team should include a leader,
generally the developer, and an urban forestry professional, a land
planner, an architect, an engineer, and others. The urban forestry

professional—called the natural resource expert—helps relate the land's natural systems to the project's development goals.

The natural resource expert is a specialist—such as an urban forester, a landscape architect, a horticulturalist, or an arborist— who is familiar with the technical aspects of tree protection, planting, and care. This person must have experience in dealing with trees on construction sites, because he or she will evaluate the site and recommend how best to protect areas targeted for tree conservation. A landscape architect—one experienced in working with trees around construction—can often serve as both a land planner and a natural resource expert.

The natural resource expert is responsible for managing all aspects of a tree conservation program (see Figure 4.1), including—

◆ showing the development team the value and condition of existing natural features and how they can enhance the built structures;
◆ helping decide which trees to save, plant, or transplant;
◆ participating in the design of preliminary through final site and construction plans that include tree conservation and planting goals and that identify areas to be augmented with new plantings;
◆ explaining to builders and subcontractors the steps to take before, during, and after construction to minimize disturbance of and stress to trees; and
◆ being available on-site during construction to monitor quality control, spot problems, and help make field adjustments to construction plans as needed.

Helping developers and builders pair up with a natural resource expert is one of the goals of the Global ReLeaf for New Communities program (see Chapter 6 for details). This developer and builder recognition program of NAHB and AMERICAN FORESTS certifies qualified natural resource experts and maintains a nationwide register, updated annually, as a resource for developers.

Other professional tree care organizations also maintain lists of qualified consultants, including the International Society of Arboriculture (ISA) and the American Society of Consulting Arborists (see Appendix). The National Arborists Association lists tree care firms, some of which include urban forestry consultants. Most

4.1 Natural Resource Expert's Role on the Development Team

- ◆ Communicate the value of existing natural features as an enhancement of built structures.
- ◆ Conduct the tree inventory.
- ◆ Prepare the tree conservation plan.
- ◆ Specify tree protection methods.
- ◆ Provide on-site supervision and field adjustments.

state Departments of Natural Resources also offer information on finding a qualified urban forestry professional locally.

The cost of hiring such an expert is generally covered by the savings achieved on other land development costs; by the enhanced marketability, sales pace, and prices resulting from a well-planned, well-treed development; and by the increased credibility awarded a firm seen as creating a quality residential environment.

Some communities now require developers to use such an expert to comply with local tree protection regulations. Although hiring an expert represents an additional cost of doing business today, many developers find they recoup what they spend on this worthwhile investment.

Site Inventory

After assembling the development team, the developer focuses on the site inventory, which assesses existing conditions—topography, soils, vegetation, water, wildlife, climate, existing buildings, roads, utilities, and easements. Also considered are cultural factors such as a community's per capita income, economic base, market demographics, historic values, and local regulatory requirements. The site's vegetation and other natural resources receive a thorough evaluation, as does all on- and off-site infrastructure needed for development.

At this point, the natural resource expert comes into play, cataloging existing trees and important natural features. To enable the development to make best use of the site's attributes, the expert helps determine how trees may enhance the overall design concept while meeting relevant regulatory requirements.

Tree Inventory

The natural resource expert prepares a tree inventory to identify trees by species, health, size, age, and location, noting particularly large, beautiful, or valuable trees, as well as those not worth saving (see Figure 4.2). Tree health is determined by the condition of the canopy, leaves, roots, bark, and trunk. The leaves of unhealthy trees tend to look pale and smaller than average for the species. Stressed

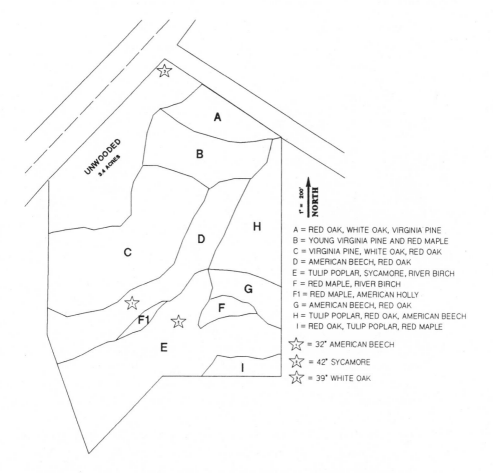

A = RED OAK, WHITE OAK, VIRGINIA PINE
B = YOUNG VIRGINIA PINE AND RED MAPLE
C = VIRGINIA PINE, WHITE OAK, RED OAK
D = AMERICAN BEECH, RED OAK
E = TULIP POPLAR, SYCAMORE, RIVER BIRCH
F = RED MAPLE, RIVER BIRCH
F1 = RED MAPLE, AMERICAN HOLLY
G = AMERICAN BEECH, RED OAK
H = TULIP POPLAR, RED OAK, AMERICAN BEECH
I = RED OAK, TULIP POPLAR, RED MAPLE

☆ = 32" AMERICAN BEECH
☆ = 42" SYCAMORE
☆ = 39" WHITE OAK

4.2 A typical tree delineation map identifies zones of predominant species on a site to help guide the design process and meet any regulatory requirements.

Source: Maryland-National Capital Park and Planning Commission, Prince George's County Planning Department.

or declining trees usually have fewer leaves than healthy trees, and their branches often contain deadwood and may be brittle and sparse. A tree that fails to leaf out at all is probably dead. The natural resource expert looks for other, more subtle signs of tree health in addition to these basics (see Figure 4.3).

Tree size is also an important consideration. Most homeowners like large, mature trees, which offer aesthetic and shade benefits and give a home an established look that smaller saplings can't yet provide.

Specimen Trees

Unusually large or well-shaped trees—called specimen trees—warrant special consideration. A tree often achieves a fine shape and form when it has been allowed to grow without competition from other trees, so saving a specimen tree may mean restricting activity within a large area of ground around a single tree or using special construction techniques to protect its root system.

The natural resource expert and the developer should discuss the merits of each specimen tree to see if protection justifies the resulting costs. Specimen trees can add real distinction and character to a neighborhood or office building. They are often hallmarks in a community and can carry more local sentimental value than whole stands or forests. Some communities have even passed ordinances protecting specimen trees of certain species.

Mixed-Aged Stands

Except in the case of specimen trees, the natural resource expert generally will try to conserve groupings of trees rather than single, isolated ones. Saving stands of trees and undergrowth greatly increases shading and cooling potential, stormwater and erosion control, wildlife benefits, visual screening, and noise reduction for homes and communities.

Stands of trees are easier to protect during construction than individual trees, and they offer better protection to soils, root systems, and plants. Then, too, groups of trees often have intertwined roots, and trees of the same species sometimes link their roots together by grafting, making tree removals tricky. In either case, bulldozing trees slated for removal can be more damaging to the remaining trees than if the trees were simply cut down. Removing all

ARBORGUARD
T R E E   S P E C I A L I S T S
For People Who Love Trees

United Parcel Service • Headquarters Campus • Tree Survey

Tree No.	Diam.	Species	Radius	Vitality	Form	Comments
1	16	White oak	10	F	25	Stressed, excessive sucker growth due to environmental conditions.
2	16	Pine	17	F	2	
3	18	White oak	24	F	25	
4	17	So. red oak	25	F	2	Unbalanced, canopy is not symmetrical
5	17	So. red oak	30	F	2	Unbalanced, canopy is not symmetrical
6	18	So. red oak	25	F	2	20% dead wood on tree
7	9	So. red oak	10	F-	2	50% of tree free of limbs from ground to first limb
8	17	So. red oak	35	F	2	
9	16	Pine	20	F+	2	Unbalanced, canopy is not symmetrical
10	17	Chestnut oak	25	P+	3+	Entire tree leans, detracting from appearance or is unsafe. 50% dead wood
11	27	Chestnut oak	40	F	2-	
12	18	White oak	25	F	2	
13	10	White oak	16	F-	2	
14	15	Poplar	25	F	2	
15	11	Chestnut oak	20	F-	2-	
16	11	Chestnut oak	12	F	2	
17	25	Chestnut oak	35	G-	1-	Possible specimen tree
18	15	Chestnut oak	25	F	2-	Unbalanced, canopy is not symmetrical

4.3 In a tree survey, every tree larger than a specified diameter is inventoried to identify tree species, health, size, age, and location.

Source: Reprinted with permission from Arborguard Tree Specialists.

the trees around an isolated specimen can also severely damage the intended survivor, leaving it more vulnerable to being toppled by windthrow. The goal should be preserving a mix of older and specimen trees along with planted or saved saplings to ensure an abundance of healthy and valuable trees for years to come.

Site Analysis

The next step is for the natural resource expert and the land planner to analyze the ecological information obtained in the site survey. Interpreting the natural elements of the site along with the cultural and regulatory conditions is called site analysis (see Figure 4.4). This analysis allows the development team to begin to see the development possibilities for the site. The team examines the threshold, or essential, elements that affect construction and factors in secondary, or nonthreshold, information.

Threshold conditions determine whether it is economically feasible to develop a site and can range from wetlands and zoning constraints to location and market demand. Nonthreshold elements affect a site but typically do not dictate whether development can occur. These can range from historic use of the property to considerations such as noise, odors, and views.

At this point, the development team prepares a summary analysis of the site, spelling out the blatantly obvious (such as the location of a stream) and the not-so-obvious (such as prevailing wind directions or the location of a fine grove of trees). Many developers perform a simple analysis of the natural and cultural aspects and regulatory context of a property before purchase, then repeat the analysis in greater detail as they become more committed to developing the parcel (see Figure 4.5).

Relating Trees to Other Site Conditions

Trees are affected by, and in turn have an effect on, three key site conditions: water, soil, and aesthetics. Since trees and undergrowth are important sediment traps and natural filters of runoff, trees near drainageways and water resources require special consideration. Trees also stabilize slopes and areas of shifting soils or sands. These areas are especially sensitive to grading, which not only

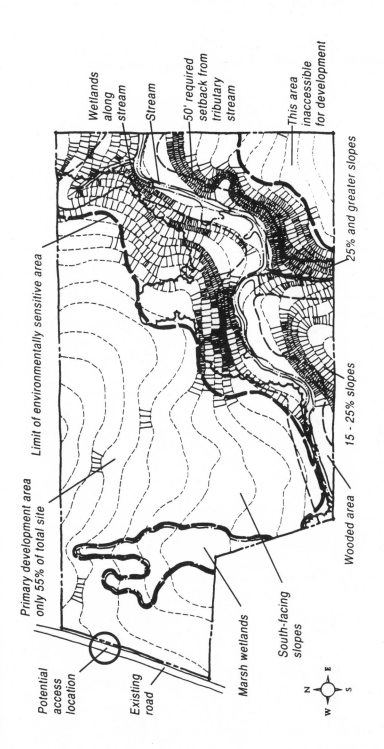

4.4 A cumulative site analysis synthesizes the site inventory data to identify opportunities and constraints. This information is used in designing the development.

Potential access location

Existing road

Marsh wetlands

South-facing slopes

Wooded area

15 - 25% slopes

25% and greater slopes

Primary development area only 55% of total site

Limit of environmentally sensitive area

Wetlands along stream

Stream

50' required setback from tributary stream

This area inaccessible for development

N E W S

Source: Frederick D. Jarvis, LDR International, Inc., *Site Planning and Community Design for Great Neighborhoods* (Washington, DC: Home Builder Press, National Association of Home Builders, 1993), p. 39.

4.5 One Developer's Analysis—The Three Phases of Land Planning

Phase One: Conceptual feasibility
Phase Two: Preliminary feasibility
Phase Three: Land development and construction planning

Site Constraints and Opportunities

A.   Environmental constraints
      1. USGS or local government soils maps
      2. FEMA or local government floodplain maps
      3. Topography
      4. Natural drainage patterns

B.   Public facilities
      1. Location of utilities
      2. Public utility capacity
      3. Road access

Government Constraints and Opportunities

A.   Zoning
B.   General subdivision regulations
      1. Tree protection
      2. Wetlands preservation
      3. Stormwater management
      4. Traffic
      5. Schools
      6. Recreation
      7. Internal roads
      8. Soils

C.   Timing and complexity of approval process, variances, and waivers

D.   Political climate for obtaining changes to standards

E.   Public involvement in approval process

F.   Bonding required

Legal Condition

A.   Title/ownership
B.   Easements/obligations
C.   Taxes, proffers, and fees

Continued

4.5 One Developer's Analysis (Continued)

Market Constraints and Opportunities

A.   General market conditions

B.   Average home sales by product, size, and price

C.   Average lot size and price

Site Plan

A.   Major roads

B.   Preliminary utilities plan

C.   Lot frontages and density

D.   Views

E.   Environmental features

F.   Spatial relationships

G.   Recreation, open space, and public space

Cash-Flow Analysis

A.   Initial budgets

B.   Initial price and absorption

C.   Financing/leveraging

D.   Profit and internal rate-of-return objectives

Note: A developer must determine the feasibility of every land-planning project. Some developers analyze every element in progressively detailed phases; each phase is tested for feasibility before proceeding to the next.

Source: Reprinted with permission from the Michael T. Rose Consulting Company, Inc., Laurel, Maryland.

affects nearby tree roots but can increase runoff into adjacent waterways.

Conserving trees near water or transplanting them to riparian sites (sites with seasonal or year-round surface water) helps protect water quality. Doing so can qualify as a best-management practice under state and federal stormwater management and water quality mandates. Saving trees in these areas often can also satisfy local ordinances' open space requirements mandating that a percentage of developed land be set aside in its natural state.

Existing soil conditions are another consideration. Topsoil is by far the richest soil on a site, having the best combination of organic matter, minerals, and structure suitable for plant growth. Most plants cannot grow in the subsurface hardpan or compacted soils of a disturbed site. Protect topsoil wherever possible, and in areas slated for construction, remove it and set it aside for use after construction is complete.

The natural resource expert helps the development team plan how to protect soil from damaging changes in its structural and chemical integrity. If soil on the development site has been previously disturbed, especially from such practices as mining, chemical dumping and storage, or compaction, the expert should assess the soil's ability to sustain plant life.

Scenic potential is also a consideration, since well-sited and aesthetically pleasing trees improve the property's appearance to homeowners and the broader community. Explore various scenarios, since aesthetics and views change from site to site and lot to lot. Ideally, the development team's plan for buildings and roads will retain valuable trees, or it may recommend selectively clearing or pruning trees to enhance a view.

Computerized Analysis

Computers are ideal tools for processing complex site and design data. Geographic Information Systems (GIS) technology offers great promise for providing a comprehensive look at both the existing and planned features of a property. The cost of GIS, however, should be considered up front. Using GIS technology requires high-quality data and computer analysis time. As this technology becomes integrated into local planning agencies and consulting firms, expect the price to drop significantly and the availability of programs to increase.

With a GIS program, the developer and the natural resource expert can use existing digital data or hard-copy maps and photos (often available through local planning agencies) as site base maps. The digital maps provide a palette on which to plot such things as significant vegetation, slopes, and water resources. Through computer simulation, lots may be divided up and moved around, and houses may be rendered for anticipated best siting among existing trees. The developer and natural resource expert can use the GIS program as a design and marketing tool to site new trees, simulate their mature sizes, and show buyers what their community will look like 20 years from now. GIS programs are often compatible with computer drawing (CAD) programs used by landscape architects and engineers.

A GIS program also can help the development team calculate the size of protection zones needed to preserve trees, wetlands, and other landscape features. With enough information about the existing site, a natural resource expert can use the program to work with engineers to include tree cover in stormwater management, street layout, and grading decisions.

AMERICAN FORESTS has developed one of the most advanced and comprehensive evaluation techniques, using GIS technology to perform a comprehensive urban ecological analysis. The Urban Forestry staff calculates the cost-benefits of tree cover as it affects water quality, stormwater management, soil erosion controls, and energy savings. Developers can use this analysis simulating different development scenarios to influence land-planning decision makers. (For more information about urban ecological analysis, contact the Urban Forestry department at AMERICAN FORESTS.)

Developing Alternatives

If development seems feasible, the design team generates and evaluates several scenarios based on the site analysis. These should include development alternatives and specific options for saving and transplanting trees, planting new trees, and obtaining variances to avoid unnecessary tree removal. Innovative site planning and lot layout options, including cluster development, are best considered at this point. Trees proposed for saving are matched against the design concept, existing regulatory constraints, and budget.

The number of trees saved hinges on the amount of root space protected from construction disturbance. This protective zone for tree roots is one of the most important planning elements for conserving trees. Most root systems grow within the top 18 inches of soil, not downward, spreading out many feet beyond the tree's crown. The natural resource expert must accurately determine the amount of space around a tree that should remain undisturbed by construction activities; this can vary depending on factors such as climate and slope. Under the best of circumstances, trees can only seal off (not heal) damage, so preventing tree injuries through good planning is the only effective way to avoid losses.

The alternatives adopted to create Bradford Ridge Apartments—an affordable-housing development in Indiana that qualified as a Global ReLeaf New Community—illustrate how changes can dramatically improve tree retention and enhance a project. Developer Brad Chambers and his team already had initial plans for a 130-unit apartment complex on a 12-acre site. Its conventional design was similar to that of a neighboring development. Faced with the scenic beauty of the heavily wooded site, Chambers saw that the original design would necessitate cutting large numbers of mature trees. Working with Global ReLeaf natural resource expert Steven Goodwin and using Goodwin's tree inventory and analysis, the team decided to redesign the complex.

On such a small property, a great deal of creativity was required to maximize tree conservation. The biggest change involved redesigning the buildings to better fit the natural contours of the land. Originally planned as two floors on slabs, the buildings were redesigned for three stories, with the first level tucked into the slopes. Smaller parking lots were also placed closer to buildings.

The end result greatly reduced grading of slopes and dramatically increased the number of retained trees. It also left natural buffers between buildings, saving large groups of trees for both privacy screening and natural views. A stormwater management pond was created for runoff and existing plantings were augmented for wildlife and recreation. These changes were well worth the extra $300,000 they cost: The completed project fits the site beautifully, stands out from the competition, reached 100 percent occupancy in less than a year, and created units with views that commanded higher prices. Bradford Ridge also serves to illustrate that higher-density development can be compatible with tree conservation efforts.

Determining Tree Options

A good tree program considers all available options—save, transplant, or plant—while keeping in mind that, in general, the more mature trees are removed, the less attractive the development is during its early years. Preserving a mix of young and old keeps the trees from all reaching maturity and declining at the same time and creates a healthier urban forest.

It is almost impossible and sometimes undesirable to retain all existing trees, except on sparsely treed properties. The natural resource expert's role is to propose other tree options, such as transplanting and planting, to augment existing trees (see Figure 4.6).

Retaining Existing Trees. The development team should draw heavily on the natural resource expert's professional knowledge of which trees provide the greatest benefits. In general, larger stands of retained trees better resist construction stresses and windthrow and offer greater aesthetic and wildlife values than isolated individuals or small strips of trees (see Figure 4.7).

Homes that are well sited among mature trees for maximum energy conservation offer another marketing advantage. But do not retain large trees very close to buildings unless the development team is committed to the careful work needed to protect them from construction impacts. Extensive design changes may be necessary—changes such as using pilings instead of slab foundations to minimize grading or using special construction equipment and techniques, such as tunneling, for utility installation. This kind of work is demanding but has been done successfully by Maryland developer Michael T. Rose and others, as described later in this chapter.

Selective Clearing. On a wooded property, the natural resource expert may suggest selective site clearing or "thinning" to benefit those trees chosen for retention. Selective clearing involves removing damaged or declining trees and undesirable species. Trees that block a special view are often also removed or pruned.

The natural resource expert should help the developer select the tree removal contractor if he or she is not equipped to do the work. A good choice is a tree care firm certified by the International Society of Arboriculture and working under the natural resource expert's supervision. Selective clearing is done gradually on heavily wooded sites, preferably at least one season prior to the beginning of construction. Trees grown in competition with each other tend to be tall and slender and, when suddenly exposed by thinning, are more prone to windthrow and leaning, regardless of species. Drastic thinning can also lead to sunburn on newly exposed bark. Gradual thinning allows the remaining trees time to develop sturdier trunks and a more even branching pattern. It also allows the bark time to adjust to the increase in sunlight.

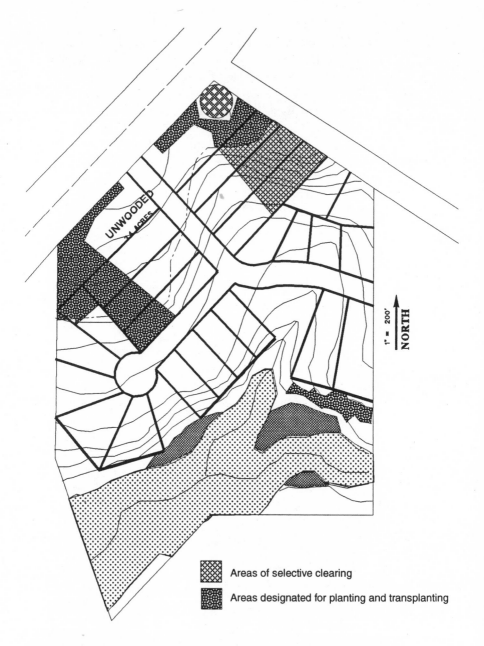

UNWOODED

1" = 200'
NORTH

Areas of selective clearing

Areas designated for planting and transplanting

4.6 This woodland conservation map shows several tree options for a site, designating areas for selective clearing and areas where new planting and replanting will occur following construction.

Source: Maryland-National Capital Park and Planning Commission, Prince George's County Planning Department.

4.7 Sample Checklist for Retaining Existing Trees

◆ Are the trees proposed for protection of a species and size appropriate for saving?

◆ Are the trees within the proposed save areas healthy and generally in good condition?

◆ Will proposed grading for the lot maintain the existing hydrology (that is, the grade changes will not make the tree-save areas significantly wetter or drier than present conditions)?

◆ Will necessary grading occur outside the proposed tree-save areas, if possible?

◆ Has adequate drainage been provided on the lot in light of tree protection areas?

◆ Are proposed utilities, such as sewer, water, and telephone and electric lines, located outside the proposed tree-save areas, if possible?

◆ Are stormwater management and erosion and sediment control structures, such as berming, silt fencing, and detention ponds, located outside the proposed tree-save areas, if possible?

Source: Maryland-National Capital Park and Planning Commission, Prince George's County Planning Department.

Transplanting Trees. Although professional tree nurseries can produce the best-quality trees, developers can save on purchasing costs by creating a tree farm on-site or nearby with either seedlings or trees transplanted from areas designated for clearing and construction. Transplanted trees can be larger than the ones most nurseries offer and generally are already acclimated to local site conditions. Using a tree spade or other equipment allows the developer to transplant the trees cost-effectively (see Figure 4.8). Trees may also be purchased and transplanted from other sites, as tree expert Steve Clark and Maryland developer Michael T. Rose have done. The natural resource expert should oversee the nursery production and transplanting process.

Oklahoma City developer David Yost's Apple Valley subdivision was carved from 160 acres that included highly eroded pastureland where many of the trees were contained in old fencerows. Yost converted a nearby site into a tree farm and moved some of the trees there during construction. He also bought small, inexpensive

4.8 Large trees can be transplanted using specialized equipment for digging and transporting.

Source: Reprinted with permission from the Michael T. Rose Consulting Company, Inc., Laurel, Maryland.

seedlings to grow at the tree farm and plant in the subdivision (see Figure 4.9).

Yost used his tree farm to full advantage, giving each Apple Valley home buyer a good-sized tree, using others to improve the quality of the site, and donating still others to the community for planting in parks and other public areas. He believes the improvements he made to Apple Valley with transplanted trees helped keep his lots selling ahead of the competition during Oklahoma's late-1980s recession.

Stock tree farms with species that are best suited to the site, whether they are native to the area or exotic (nonnative). Be aware that some community tree ordinances prohibit certain exotics and specify that replanting be done with native species. Native species help retain the site's original character and can link the development to adjacent natural areas.

Today's technology allows even trees of considerable size to be moved safely. Such trees can be transplanted before construction begins for use in prominent areas such as entranceways or where

4.9 *Establishing an on-site tree farm can save on purchasing costs and provide home buyers and communities with much larger, more attractive trees sooner than nursery stock would.*

Source: Apple Valley, Oklahoma City, Oklahoma. Reprinted with permission from David T. Yost, Future Investments Company.

screening is desirable. During construction, any previously added plantings will need as much careful protection as the trees that grew there originally.

New Plantings. Many developers have their natural resource expert help select new plantings to increase the number and variety of trees on a site. If planted correctly and cared for, healthy, well-grown nursery trees have an excellent chance of becoming strong, healthy assets to the community's ecosystem. However, developing on particularly wet or dry sites or on acidic or sweet soil (soil with a low or a high pH) will severely limit tree choices. Development plans can also affect soil conditions and thus tree selection. The expert should be aware of these factors and advise the developer accordingly.

Most people know the trees they select should suit their climatic zone. But many don't realize they should look to local or regional sources when buying species that grow over a wide range of climatic conditions. For example, white oak (*Quercus alba*) grows

from the Northeast to the Gulf Coast, but seedlings raised in an
Ohio nursery may not thrive in the hotter, more humid conditions
of southern Georgia.

In certain areas of the country, water conservation is another
important factor. Xeriscaping is a landscaping approach that emphasizes appropriate plant choices and careful planning to address limited water availability. Lawns require high water use and do not
return anywhere near the benefits that trees do. A newly planted
tree needs only 10 to 15 gallons of water a week; even in arid climates some of this will come from rainfall. Giving drought-tolerant
tree species precedence over lawns can produce considerably
cooler, more pleasant communities.

When selecting individual trees for purchase, a different set of
factors applies. (*Growing Greener Cities* describes these in greater
detail; see References.) Healthy roots are essential; reject any trees
with kinked or broken (as opposed to cleanly cut) roots. Certain
nursery practices can encourage a particularly damaging problem
called girdling roots, in which a root grows around a tree's base
in a stranglehold. Avoid selecting these types of trees for a new
development.

Regardless of size, a tree should have a rootball large enough to
properly support and provide for it. The natural resource expert
should follow the American Association of Nurserymen's nursery
stock standards for rootball size. Container-grown stock is the easi-
est to evaluate; field-grown stock that has been dug for selling is
more difficult. The natural resource expert will recognize trees that
have lost too much of their roots in the digging process; generally,
the roots should be cut only where they are thinner than a finger.

Examine trees to ensure that they don't have codominant leaders (more than one dominant, upright stem or trunk), crossed or rub-
bing branches, or insect or disease problems. Also reject trees with
wounds from damage or improper pruning. When arranging purchase, the developer should reserve the right to inspect and reject
flawed or damaged trees. The developer's natural resource expert
can visit the tree source and select and tag trees to be shipped to the
project before digging. Careless shipping can damage good trees en
route to a site, so the developer should have the right to reject them
up to the point when they're received at the site.

Recycling Tree Resources. When existing trees don't fit into the development plan, they can still be put to good use. New Community designee C.P. Morgan recycled wood products from trees he was unable to save or transplant in his Lake Forest subdivision in Carmel, Indiana. Branches and smaller trunks were chipped to mulch later plantings and a nature trail, and a dead tree in the nature area was carefully preserved upright as a home for woodpeckers. Note, however, that dead trees should not be saved for wildlife where they will pose a hazard to people or structures.

C.P. Morgan also gave scrap cedar to the local Audubon Society, which built birdhouses for the nature trail. The benefit was twofold. Not only was the wood put to use for the environment, the developer was able to build a positive relationship with a local environmental group.

Using chipped wood and clippings will help minimize soil compaction and reduce water runoff during construction. Larger limbless trunks, called boles, are useful as lumber, fence rails, or firewood. A community recycling center or parks department may also have uses for excess wood products. The natural resource expert can facilitate converting removed trees into usable products.

Trees as Part of the Regulatory Process

Tree Ordinances. Ordinances provide communities with a legislative means of protecting trees. Some also contain provisions that may hamper a developer's ability to work with the existing trees. The best tree conservation ordinances focus on minimizing the negative impacts of construction and improving the local environmental and aesthetic resources. Such ordinances are based on tree banking, a concept that emphasizes conserving stands of trees rather than individuals and weighs the costs and benefits of mature trees on a site versus the costs and benefits of planting new trees.

Faced with heavy tree losses in the fast-growing Atlanta metropolitan area, Fulton County, Georgia, enacted a tree conservation ordinance that drew on the tree-banking concept. Rather than using preexisting site conditions to prescribe preservation or replacement mandates, Fulton County established a point system that converts the diameter inches of a tree's basal area to "density units." Developers must provide a finished project with a prescribed density of trees per acre. The developer has the flexibility to combine saving, planting, and transplanting, using variously sized trees. And planting new trees off-site (known as off-site mitigation) is acceptable when the developing site is not a practical choice for conserving or planting trees.

Fulton County's tree conservation ordinance is precise in intent, enforceability, and appeals process but deliberately vague in general requirements. This allows the urban forester to grant compromises without requiring lengthy appeals or redrafting the ordinance. It prevents developers of heavily forested properties from facing exorbitant replanting mandates, and—at the other end of the spectrum—requires site improvement from developers who work with degraded or treeless properties. The ordinance also takes an educational and cooperative tack, providing developers with hands-on information on how to minimize tree damage.

When do tree conservation ordinances hinder rather than help? Some overemphasize saving large trees, ignoring the fact that some smaller species are more valuable than others twice their size. And focusing too heavily on size may force developers to preserve declining giants that are dying from decades or even centuries of cumulative damage. Other tree ordinances require developers to replace trees on a one-for-one or even two- or three-for-one basis. These standards can prove impractical on-site since buildings and parking lots take up space that presumably was previously forested. These standards may not make sense environmentally, either, since they can lead to overcrowding as the newly planted trees grow.

The intent of most tree conservation ordinances is to save some desirable trees endangered by construction and to balance out the removal of others with new trees. Ordinances differ chiefly in how many trees developers must replant and where this must occur. Ordinances that permit off-site mitigation can allow developers an opportunity to provide trees to a local school, park, or forest restoration area, resulting in a favorable partnership between the developer and the community.

The best approach is to get involved while ordinances are being drafted. Developers who have conserved trees with the help of a natural resource expert stand a good chance of helping create a flexible ordinance that reflects both sound urban forestry science and legitimate development and construction concerns. If an unduly restrictive ordinance is already in place, developers should try to negotiate for flexibility using specific counterproposals that demonstrate how they could achieve more sensitive development.

Innovative Site-Planning Options

Most communities have other regulatory requirements that can unwittingly hamper tree protection goals. Local zoning and subdivision standards often effectively force developers to remove trees to comply with road, grading, lot clearing, and utility and setback minimums. These standards are sometimes excessive, and as discussed later in this chapter, negotiations with local planning and public works agencies may allow more mature trees to be saved without compromising safety.

Conventional zoning itself is often a constraint because it typically requires lots of approximately equal sizes, leaving little incentive or even room for greenspace or groupings of trees. Cluster development is a more flexible site-planning technique that can save more trees, but it often requires special approval from local governments.

The natural resource expert can help identify areas where waivers are warranted to preserve more trees *and* reduce development costs. He or she can also help the developer present the case to local regulatory authorities—an excellent first opportunity for the developer to alert the community to his or her desire to conserve trees and build with nature.

Zoning and Subdivision Ordinance Waivers. Maryland developer Michael T. Rose has pioneered some of the tree-saving techniques discussed in this book and has negotiated for flexibility in local regulations that affect tree conservation efforts. For his planned community of Northridge in Bowie, Maryland, Rose obtained reductions in road-width requirements (see Figure 4.10) and slope ratios (three-to-one reduced to two-to-one) (see Figure 4.11). On both counts, Rose argued, allowing steeper natural slopes and reducing road widths did not compromise residents' safety. In fact, studies have shown wide roads increase the incidence of speeding; narrow roads visually influence drivers to slow down.

After inspecting the rural site, the local and county planning boards approved the changes. These two waivers alone freed up much valuable land, and the development team was able to fit homes into the rolling, wooded site, creating a more attractive

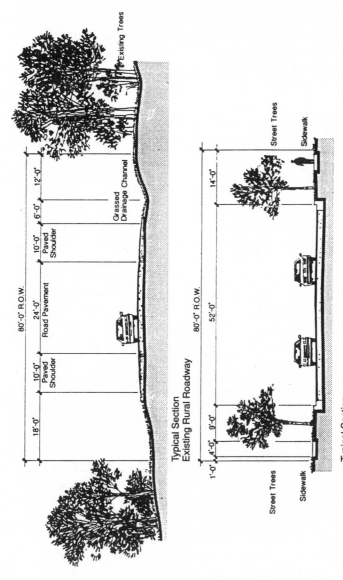

Typical Section
Existing Rural Roadway

80'-0" R.O.W.

18'-0" | 10'-0"
Paved
Shoulder | 24'-0"
Road Pavement | 10'-0"
Paved
Shoulder | 6'-0" | 12'-0"

Grassed
Drainage Channel

Existing Trees

Typical Section
Prince George's County Proposed Upgraded Road

80'-0" R.O.W.

1'-0" | 4'-0" | 9'-0" | 52'-0" | 14'-0"

Street Trees

Sidewalk

Street Trees

Sidewalk

4.10 *Typical design for roadways, curbs and gutters, sidewalks, and street tree plantings maximizes hardscape and minimizes tree space (bottom). An alternative design narrows roadways, provides natural drainage, and saves existing stands of trees (top). (Note that R.O.W. means right-of-way.)*

Source: Reprinted with permission from the Michael T. Rose Consulting Company, Inc., Laurel, Maryland.

development. The waivers also reduced the amount of grading and saved on such typical land development costs as clearing and grubbing (see Figure 4.11). Reducing the size of the housing-pad shelf from 20 feet to 4 feet for single-family detached homes and at the ends of townhome complexes allowed Rose to save even more trees and to do so much closer to the houses. This kept significant naturalized areas as visual buffers between the homes, saved on landscaping costs, and increased the value of the property for buyer and seller alike.

With an understanding of the ingredients necessary for long-term tree health, Rose also recommended grassed drainage swales where possible and smaller cul-de-sacs with planted islands in the centers. These reduce stormwater runoff, as more water is absorbed directly into the soil. Boardwalks on pilings can also provide access with minimal disturbance to the environment; these were used along Northridge's nature trail.

Grassed drainage swales look more natural than curbs, gutters, and storm drains and—with appropriate approvals—can be used in low- to moderate-density developments to help preserve and replenish local groundwater, an increasingly important issue. Grassed

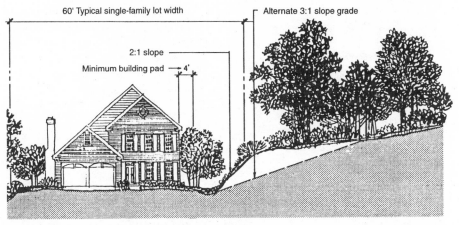

4.11 The Northridge development illustrates how a two-to-one slope will save more existing vegetation than the more conventional three-to-one slope, which disturbs more of the natural topography and thus removes more trees.

Source: Reprinted with permission from the Michael T. Rose Consulting Company, Inc., Laurel, Maryland.

drainage swales can also reduce construction costs. And planting islands in cul-de-sacs helps shade cars and hot pavement, reduce noise and runoff, and increase privacy for nearby homes.

At his Solomon's Landing project in Solomons, Maryland, Rose obtained permission to erect the buildings on pilings to reduce grading and clearing and thus save more trees. The land underneath the buildings was then covered by a mixture of rocks, filtration cloth, and oyster shells to filter runoff; this system relied on sheet flow infiltration rather than stormwater detention ponds, further reducing the area slated for clearing.

Cluster Development. Cluster development is a site-planning technique that allows developers to group lots and structures on one portion of a site, leaving the rest open and undeveloped, while achieving the same net density on the site as a conventional layout (see Figure 4.12). Cluster development offers a major site-planning

4.12 Clustering homes can save more existing trees, open space, and other natural features on-site and save on utility installation costs without affecting net density.

Source: Reprinted with permission from Frederick D. Jarvis, LDR International, Inc.

advantage that can save large numbers of trees and other natural areas while achieving significant cost savings in utility installation.

The first Global ReLeaf New Community, the Lake Forest subdivision in Carmel, Indiana, took advantage of that city's existing ordinance allowing cluster development in place of a conventional lot layout. The Lake Forest site contained a 7-acre pond and a 5-acre woodland on a 60-acre soybean field. Carmel's existing S-1 residential zoning regulations would have allowed for 150 homesites (12,000 square foot minimum), but the design would have necessitated the destruction of its natural features.

A cluster development saved not only the most desirable natural features—the pond and the woodland—but allowed developer C.P. Morgan to create two additional ponds and ultimately preserve more than 15 percent of the total development site for neighborhood common areas. And Morgan still built 148 clustered homes on lots of at least 6,000 square feet, virtually the same number of units that would have been produced under a conventional lot layout with no common greenspace.

In spite of its advantages, however, many local governments have either not allowed cluster development or have effectively discouraged its use through unnecessarily complex and lengthy review and approval procedures. Too often, it is mistakenly confused with high-density development, even though it does not increase the allowable density on a site. Developers and their resource experts should help local officials see the benefits of expressly allowing the use of cluster development without special approval.

Density Bonuses. Some communities offer developers density bonuses or incentives used separately or in conjunction with cluster development. Density bonuses allow a developer to subdivide a property into more house lots than conventional zoning permits. This can help the developer justify setting aside a portion of the site as greenspace in exchange for increasing the return on the remaining property. Some communities associate increased density with the loss of an area's rural character, but the resulting open space or greenway may do more to preserve rural character than a standard layout of larger, near-treeless lots.

Utilities. Since grading and utility installation are essential to development, the goal is to minimize the areas exposed to these practices when conserving trees. At a minimum, developers should try to coordinate plans as closely with utility companies as they do with all other project subcontractors.

Many utility companies have recently shown a greater willingness to work with developers on alternative ways to site or install utilities and minimize tree disturbance. Innovative techniques include installing utilities in a shared right-of-way or even a single common trench and relocating utilities to the front of lots so more trees can be saved behind homes (see Figure 4.13). Using these techniques often requires more organizational than engineering skills. Not only must these be coordinated with the various utility companies, but local government approval—or even variances— are usually needed, since local building codes require certain vertical and horizontal separation of utilities. (Consult NAHB or your local city or county engineer for more information.)

Mark Boyce, Chief Operating Officer of C.P. Morgan Company in Carmel, Indiana, has worked successfully with utility companies to coordinate locating sanitary sewer and water lines in one utility corridor. He notes that the coordination adds time to the process, but that "planning the utility corridors and siting

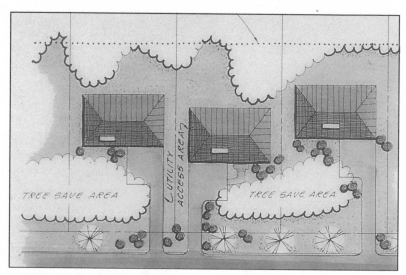

4.13 Creating a shared right-of-way for utilities between homes minimizes soil and vegetation disturbance.

Source: Reprinted with permission from the Michael T. Rose Consulting Company, Inc., Laurel, Maryland.

transformers allowed us to site individual homes while retaining existing tree stands."

Telephone and electric wires may also be placed underground and tunneled rather than trenched, as described in Chapter 3. Installing underground utilities is more expensive than conventional overhead wiring, but it is generally less disruptive to trees, and using a single common trench can cut the cost somewhat. Many home buyers are also attracted to a "wire-free" house lot—not to mention a wire-free house lot that is well treed. Protect wiring for electrical and telephone lines with plastic conduit, since it tends to deteriorate more quickly than wiring for other utilities. It is important to try to verify that the wires are functional; this prevents the developer from having to dig up and replace new utility lines.

Planning for overhead wire installation requires close coordination with utility companies, taking into account not just the existing trees but their future growth and any later plantings. Protective coatings on overhead wires provide an alternative to trimming tree limbs. The natural resource expert can provide information on the best trees for planting near overhead lines.

Master Planning Process

After examining several development scenarios and alternatives, a developer settles on one and begins the master planning stage. The chosen option is designed in three levels of scale and detail, each increasing in complexity. The first is a concept master plan; the second, design plans; and the third and most detailed, construction documents. At this point, detailed decisions are made about where to place buildings, roads, and utilities in light of resource constraints and potential, the overall development goals, and available budget. Building in concert with a site's natural resources makes these details all the more important.

The protection areas proposed by the natural resource expert are incorporated into the overall plan. He or she will try to find the best way to minimize the impact of construction on the site's natural resources and to use those resources to enhance the buildings. Any changes made now—and some will still need to be made—can impact the future health of the site's trees. The natural resource expert must judge how the trees will react to construction changes and suggest design and construction techniques to protect them.

Master Plan

The master plan is often a single document that shows the whole development without much detail. It shows the overall scheme for the selected development option and guides a more detailed design of buildings and site improvements in the next stage of planning. The master plan shows forested areas and other important natural features in relation to all the planned built features on-site. Detailed tree placement and tree protection zones are shown in the design and construction plans.

Site or Design Plans

The second phase of master planning is considerably more detailed. The development team has a clear understanding of what is planned, construction and conservation areas have been determined, and all significant planned and existing elements—building areas, driveways, streets, drainage systems, utilities, rock ridges, waterways, and trees—are now shown in more accurate detail. The site plans allow project engineers, architects, and the natural resource expert to draw the development scheme at a more detailed scale, identifying potential problems and opportunities.

Each page or sheet of drawings at this stage likely will represent only one element of the total development. For example, one page might show grading, another stormwater details. The site plans include all trees scheduled for protection or removal as well as areas to be planted or replanted after construction is complete.

Construction Documents

Construction documents consist of plans and specifications that together present the exact dimensions and locations of everything to be constructed on a site. The plans show the details graphically; written specifications or "specs" supplement the drawing with additional instructions and technical data. Construction documents further detail the type and quality of pavers and how to place and grade paver sections so they are compatible with the root zones of preserved trees growing next to the road.

The construction plans should address each of a development's components: clearing, grading and drainage, utility installation (separated into water and sewer systems; lighting; telephone and cable television lines; and electrical, gas, and oil lines), buildings, hardscape installation, tree conservation plan, landscaping, and irrigation.

Just as construction documents must include the most precise level of detail for a storm drain or an intersection, so must they accurately detail and specify the steps and techniques necessary to preserve or add natural elements. For natural elements, landscape construction plans typically reflect details such as mulching and irrigation.

Construction documents for each development component should relate to tree conservation goals. They should also state how the site supervisor will implement the tree conservation goals during each phase of construction.

Grading. The best site planning minimizes grading. The less grading done, the greater is the area available for preservation in a natural state and the less money the developer has to spend on grading, drainage systems, restoration of soil, and relandscaping. Land left with its natural vegetation intact is better able to resist erosion and thus reduce the need for costly control measures.

As Brad Chambers and other developers have shown, siting roads and buildings to follow natural contours helps minimize grading. Keeping parking lot sizes and road widths to a minimum is also beneficial. Construction plans and specifications should reflect details (such as protective fencing and silt fences) needed to minimize the impact of grading and keep grading equipment away from tree protection zones. If grading areas are separated by a tree protection zone, a path is needed for the grading equipment. The details of this path are shown in the construction documents for grading.

Utilities. The natural resource expert should review the location of utility trenches on construction documents, coordinate with utility companies to achieve the best placement, observe trenching or tunneling, ensure quality control of any necessary root pruning, and watch over tree protection zones.

Building. One of the innovative design alternatives mentioned earlier reduces the building pad to retain more trees closer to the buildings. This kind of work must be planned and executed with precision if it is to succeed. Details of moving, storing, and lifting supplies must be spelled out and actual construction closely observed by the natural resource expert.

The natural resource expert and developer also should designate a special washout area for contractors to rinse out cement or concrete trucks or tools. Designate areas for activities that should occur away from the root protection zone, such as for "cookers" that hold roof tar, chemical and fuel storage, and parking (to avoid fluid leaks into sensitive soil), as well as for stockpiling soil and building materials and for crews to eat and take breaks.

Hardscape Installation. Because tree roots and paved surfaces can have adverse effects on each other, it's best to locate paved surfaces outside the designated root protection zone whenever possible. This allows for some growth while the tree begins to redirect other roots away from the roadbed.

Where road or sidewalk surfaces are needed under a tree canopy, developers can use unmortared porous pavers, bricks, or flagstone rather than concrete or asphalt. Unmortared stone or brick pavers cause less soil compaction than paving, maintain soil chemistry, and allow water, air, and nutrients to pass to tree roots. Boardwalks or bridging can span root zones without harming the trees' roots (see Figure 4.14).

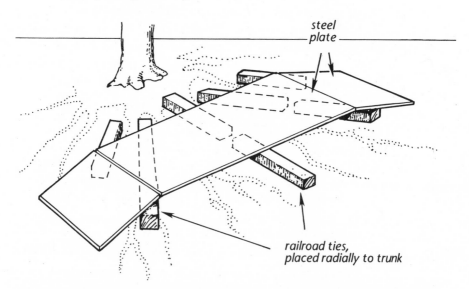

4.14 Boardwalks or bridging can be used to span root zones and carry construction traffic with minimal disturbance to roots.

Source: Drawing is copyrighted by, and reproduced with permission of, the Minnesota Extension Service, University of Minnesota, from its publication FO-6135, *Protecting Trees from Construction Damage* (revised 1995).

In some cases, local laws may mandate that soils be loosened or injected with air to counter compaction and restore permeability on heavily worked sites. The natural resource expert can ascertain if this is needed, regardless of whether it is required by local regulations.

Tree Conservation Plan. Because tree care and conservation are preventive in nature, the process of planning for trees means anticipating problems as much as possible. The developer, natural resource expert, and design team should work together on a tree conservation plan as part of the construction documents.

A tree conservation plan details how to incorporate existing trees and natural resources into the development, focusing on preventing damage as much as possible. The plan will list details on selective clearing as well as actions planned to prepare trees to better withstand construction impacts, such as mulching, fertilizing, pruning, or thinning.

The plan should show "footprints" of trees slated for conservation: the trunk location with its elevation marked, the diameter of each tree's canopy, and the root protection zone. Locations should be confirmed with exact measurements and the trees numbered to correspond with the tree inventory done in the site survey. Because the natural elements of a site are so intertwined, protective measures planned to conserve not only the trees but supporting soils and natural features such as bodies of water are delineated in the plan.

Preparing the Trees. A developer may prepare trees to better withstand stresses by fertilizing them well in advance of beginning construction. A good fertilization program done with selective thinning can help even more. As poorer-quality or unwanted trees are removed, the remaining trees can use fertilizer to considerable advantage. Phosphorous can help them produce healthy new roots, and nitrogen can allow tree crowns to fill in the overhead gaps created when competing trees are removed.

Unfortunately, felling unwanted trees in the midst of a crowded grove or patch of forest can badly damage trees a developer intends to save. Carelessly dropping trees into each other can shatter crowns and strip protective bark, disfiguring desirable trees and opening the way for disease and insect infestations.

Pruning is another preparatory measure that can benefit trees. (See *Growing Greener Cities*, listed in the References section, for more detail.) A desirable tree that has grown a lopsided crown in response to competition may need to have some limbs removed to help it withstand winds after surrounding trees are removed or to improve its aesthetics. Branches that begin extremely close to the ground may need to be removed for safety, aesthetics, or even access by the homeowner.

Mulching can also make a profound difference in efforts to protect existing trees, buffering the soil from a certain amount of compaction. Realen Homes of Pennsylvania discovered that 12 to 18 inches of chipped, not shredded, mulch spread around the base of protected trees is quite effective at preventing compaction damage caused by vehicles and equipment. While mulch is not a substitute for root protection zones and can prove detrimental to trees if mounded up against their trunks and bark, it can have a particularly positive effect in preserving roots and soils at the margins of construction activity. On a site that undergoes any clearing or grubbing, a developer can save money by making at least some of the needed mulch from shredded small trees, brush, and stumps of removed trees.

Landscape Plan. Even when native understory plants are preserved along with groups of trees, most developers will want to add new trees, shrubs, and groundcover to augment existing vegetation. This must be done carefully, as the watering requirements of introduced plants can harm existing trees, especially natives in arid climates. The landscape documents should show new planting areas, noting species, quantities, stock size, and location of all plant materials. Other details should include irrigation, fencing, fountains, landscape lighting, and mulch areas.

Landscaping is typically designed by landscape architectural firms and installed by landscape contractors. The landscaping design and installation are done in consultation with the natural resource expert. It is just as important to familiarize the landscape architect and contractor with the development plans as it is the other subcontractors.

Correct Planting Method. To plant a tree, prepare a planting area no deeper than the rootball but three to five times wider (see Figure 4.15). Loosening the soil allows the roots to grow more swiftly into the native soil, anchoring the tree sooner against persistent or violent winds and setting the stage for healthy canopy growth. All green organic matter (fresh leaves and grass) and chopped roots should be removed from the backfill soil before planting and the tree's roots loosened and spread out.

Use the native soil to backfill holes unless it is both poor and distinctly heavier in clay content. Heavy surrounding soil acts as a giant clay pot, forcing the tree's new root tips to travel around the edges of the hole without ever escaping into the surrounding

The old way.

4.15 The correct planting method for trees requires a planting area three to five times wider than the rootball.

Source: AMERICAN FORESTS.

ground. Heavy clay soils in particular may need amending with composted manures or peat. Sand is an excellent drainage material but a poor amendment because it binds with clay soils to create a rock-hard, cement-like aggregate, killing or stunting the tree planted in it.

The trees will need water immediately, but avoid the old practice of tamping or packing down the soil except for very fine sandy soils; a simple, thorough watering will settle the soil sufficiently. The natural resource expert will recommend an appropriate fertilizer program and schedule for the newly planted trees, but fertilizing during the first year can burn tender new roots. After a year, trees benefit most from a balanced, timed-release fertilizer, applied according to the manufacturer's directions. If bark or wood chip mulch is used, apply higher-nitrogen fertilizer; the microorganisms that break down wood mulch intercept nitrogen from the soil, making it less available to tree roots.

Contrary to popular belief, staking is not a good idea except on the windiest sites. Letting a flexible young tree move with the wind results in a sturdier trunk. If winds are actually rocking the tree in its planting hole, plan to stake the tree with a flexible material such as an old bicycle inner tube or garden hose. Some nurseries and garden centers now carry flexible holders specifically designed for tree staking.

In any case, staking must be a strictly temporary measure to avoid strangling the tree. Innumerable trees are killed every year because no one remembers to go back and remove fasteners. Plan to remove the stakes six months to one year later—two years later at the most. Difficult sites—particularly arid sites in the western United States—may need staking for up to five years. Check stake fasteners twice each year to ensure that they are not injuring the tree.

Mulch is virtually essential for any planting. It serves a multitude of purposes: It keeps sunlight from destroying organic elements in the soil, conserves soil moisture for the tree's roots, provides micronutrients and organic matter needed for tree growth, reduces competition from weeds and grasses, serves as a physical barrier to lawn mowers and weed trimmers, and provides a visual barrier to keep people from walking too close and compacting nearby soil.

There are basically two types of mulch: organic and inorganic. Organic mulches are made from bark, leaves, and other plant products that decompose over time. Inorganic mulches are made from pebbles, stone, crushed brick, and other long-lasting materials. Inorganic mulches provide the protective benefits of mulch and last longer than organic mulches, which break down into the soil. However, organic mulches have the added benefit of releasing nutrients to plant roots. Incidentally, compost made up of decomposed organic materials works best when mixed into the soil rather than applied to the surface as a mulch.

Irrigation for Maintenance. Even in the rainiest parts of the country, a newly planted tree will require supplemental watering in its first year. In fact, irrigation systems are a necessary part of the landscape documents. Drip irrigation and other subterranean or ground-level watering systems deliver virtually all water directly to the plant's root zone and so are preferable to sprinklers and sprayers, which can promote fungal diseases in flowers and shrubs by wetting sensitive leaves and blooms. They are also less expensive and easier to install than conventional systems, though they do not last as long. Drip/subterranean irrigation systems are best for trees and plants that need supplemental watering for only their first few years and are unsuitable for watering lawns. Computer controllers using programmable microchips are now available to regulate the irrigation system to meet individual plant needs and control water use and timing for maximum efficiency.

A general horticultural rule of thumb is that trees need an inch of rainfall per week during their growing season—the equivalent of 750 gallons of water per 1,000 square feet of root space. Stressed trees in dry conditions need water once a week; trees in sandy soils should receive the same amount of water but broken into two weekly watering treatments. The great exception: the Southwest, where native trees are adapted to dry summers with many rainless weeks. Watering these native trees is often a death sentence.

If the development site is large, consider using a tree care or landscaping firm to water conserved trees during construction. Some trees may also need nutrient, pesticide, or fungicide sprayings.

Conclusion

The master planning process brings together all foreseeable details for the project and shows how the elements relate to each other (see Figure 4.16). This process must involve the developer, the natural resource expert, and the full design and engineering team. Including the tree conservation and landscape plan as part of the master plan not only helps the developer, design team, and natural resource expert understand the design intent but is absolutely essential for helping contractors and subcontractors implement the plan successfully.

4.16 Tree Conservation as Part of the Development Process

- ◆ Assemble the development team.
- ◆ Conduct a site inventory.
- ◆ Prepare a site analysis using information gathered in the inventory.
- ◆ Develop design alternatives.
    - —Choose the most appropriate combination of retaining existing trees, selective clearing, transplanting, and planting new trees based on the site analysis.
    - —Evaluate design options in light of tree ordinance and other requirements and the possibility of obtaining waivers.
    - —Consider innovative site-planning techniques that would conserve more trees.
- ◆ Develop a master plan.
- ◆ Develop design or site plans.
- ◆ Develop detailed construction documents.
    - —Grading
    - —Utilities
    - —Building
    - —Hardscape
    - —Tree conservation plan (for existing trees)
    - —Landscape plan (for new trees)

Chapter 5

The Construction Process

B uilders and subcontractors need to know up front that trees and natural resources are not considered obstacles, but rather an integral part of the development plan. All the careful planning and preparations by the developer, natural resource expert, and design team won't matter if the construction team and builders are not educated about both tree conservation goals and process. One mistake at any point during construction could kill a tree targeted for preservation.

Shared Goals

The natural resource expert and the developer should work together to educate the construction team. The natural resource expert is a logical choice for presenting much of the information, but the developer needs to take the lead in communicating his or her commitment to conservation goals to the entire construction team. A meeting or two with the general contractor or builders, followed by a meeting on-site with all subcontractors, is usually adequate (see Figure 5.1).

For its projects, Realen Homes of Pennsylvania created a formal training course and manual on caring for trees during construction, written in conjunction with the Morris Arboretum of the University of Pennsylvania. Subcontractors are required to take the course and accept responsibility for their employees; firms that refuse are dropped from consideration.

5.1 The developer must communicate the tree conservation goals and process to all members of the construction team.

Source: First site plan review by the original Winterset planning and sales team, Winterset Park, Lee's Summit, Missouri. Reprinted with permission from G. David Gale, F.E.L. Lands.

Handing out a short training manual or group of documents that includes illustrations of concepts and techniques will help construction crew members. But this is not a substitute for an on-site information session. A lesson in tree physiology should lead into basics about the site's existing features, building and conservation goals, and what is planned to accomplish those goals. This includes explaining how subcontractors are to use equipment and accomplish tasks while respecting tree protection zones.

Don't entrust tree conservation goals to the construction team's memory alone. The tree conservation plan should specify fencing and signage to alert workers to the location of protected zones. Signs and fencing help protect the tree's canopy, roots, and bark and prevent coincidental root damage and suffocation caused by compacted soil. Signs made of metal or durable plastic can be posted to demarcate the edges of tree protection zones (see Figure 5.2). Brightly colored ribbon tape is sometimes used to indicate

5.2 Tree protection signage identifies tree protection zones and alerts workers to them.

Source: Photograph of Northridge, Bowie, Maryland, by Debra L. Bassert, NAHB.

those zones, though this tape can be easily broken and does not replace fencing.

Fencing should consist of chain-link or multiple strands of heavy-gauge wire, preferably barbed, secured with posts and made visible with brightly colored flagging (see Figure 5.3). Such sturdy fencing is more likely to be noticed if a bulldozer or truck accidentally knocks it down. If possible, the crew should install the fencing and signs, under the natural resource expert's direction, to give them a sense of attachment and ownership. Drivers and equipment operators should know to immediately reerect any portion of fence or signs they knock down.

The natural resource expert will provide quality control for protected areas and assist with last-minute change orders and field adjustments. Tree conservation goals may require the use of smaller or specialized equipment (see Figure 5.4). Smaller dozers, special "hydro-axes" (see the discussion on clearing in the next section), wide-track dozers, tunneling devices for utilities, and rubber-

5.3 *Protective fencing and mulch surround tree protection zones.*

Source: Reprinted with permission from the Michael T. Rose Consulting Company, Inc., Laurel, Maryland.

wheeled equipment make it possible to do exacting work in tight spaces and allow construction to occur with a minimum of disturbance to the natural environment.

Coordinating Construction Activity

Once the natural resource expert makes a final check of all construction documents and specs and the subcontractors have signed off on construction procedures and penalty clauses, site work can begin.

Clearing

Before clearing begins, trees that will stay are usually marked with a cloth or plastic wrapper and fenced off for protection. Many people also choose to mark trees slated for removal, usually with a spray-painted symbol on the trunk. Place tree protection signage before clearing begins.

Urban forester Steve Clark minimizes environmental impact during clearing by using a hydro-ax instead of a bulldozer when possible. This 600-pound blade spins at 1,000 revolutions per minute, cutting vegetation and small trees, grinding them into mulch, and leaving the mulch in place to protect the cleared soil. Once the trees are felled and removed, the stumps can be extracted with a stump grinder. On wet soils, wide-track dozers can pull stump grinders to avoid creating deep ruts. Stump grindings make excellent mulch either separately or mixed with other chipped organic materials.

It's best not to use bulldozers to remove trees, but if one must be used, use the smallest one possible, and spread mulch to a depth of 2 to 6 inches along its path to re-

5.4 Special equipment allows greater maneuverability in tight spaces, minimizing soil disturbance during construction.

Source: Reprinted with permission from the Michael T. Rose Consulting Company, Inc., Laurel, Maryland.

duce the amount of topsoil compacted or destroyed. Chipped organic wastes can protect soils along vehicle paths and footpaths and in material storage areas. On small sites or individual lots, it's best to hand-clear trees with a chain saw. Leave the understory growth in tree protection areas; it helps prevent erosion, intercept stormwater, and provide wildlife habitat.

Grading

Preserving existing trees and their supporting soil and hydrology during development means minimizing the amount of grading and drainage required. It also means minimizing the length of time that graded soils sit exposed, requiring a crew that is both skilled and careful. In grading areas, stockpile removed topsoil for landscaping. Do not pile the soil in a root protection zone, nor close enough to a waterway so that rain washes it into riparian zones. Leaving more areas on a site undisturbed can sometimes present a challenge for developers. Developer Michael T. Rose has solved the problem of where to place extra fill by using it to create ballfields within his developments.

If at all possible, avoid grading within a root protection zone. If the natural grade around a tree or group of trees designated for protection must be disturbed, take special measures, such as those described in the following paragraphs, to ensure tree survival.

Reconsider doing any grading that involves cutting one or more large roots; the natural resource expert can determine whether the tree can survive the cut. Even if it can survive, a major root cut can leave a tree permanently vulnerable to being blown over. If the roots are cut, use sharp saws that have been disinfected and have the work monitored closely by the natural resource expert.

Lowered Grades Near Trees

Lowering the grade in a tree's root zone will kill the tree. To preserve a tree within these areas, use a retaining wall to create an "island" at the roots' existing soil level. If a sloping grade is planned that would raise soil levels on one side of a tree and cut roots and lower the grade on the other side, the natural resource expert may opt instead to build a tree well (a retaining wall that completely surrounds a tree) and retaining wall on the side where the grade will be raised (see Figure 5.5). In either case, the retaining wall should skirt the tree's root zone if at all possible.

Whether or not roots are cut, space is needed between the grade cut and the retaining wall for filling in native soil. Concrete retaining walls will leach alkali and lower soil acidity and can harm trees and shrubs—especially acid-loving plants such as dogwoods, azaleas, and certain oaks. For this reason, natural materials such as wood or stone are often used instead of concrete.

Raised Grades Near Trees

Raising the grade within a tree's root zone presents a different set of problems, as outlined in Chapter 3. A retaining wall or even a tree well is almost always required around the desired tree to prevent suffocation (see Figure 5.6). Raise the soil level at the base of

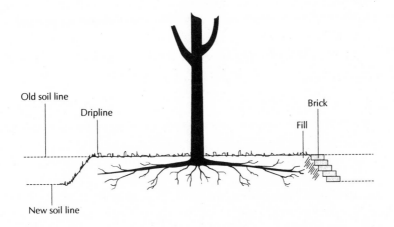

5.5 *Two methods of lowering the grade around trees: an island of existing soil held by a retaining wall (right) and a sloping grade (left). At a minimum, lower the grades outside the dripline of the tree and allow adequate root space to accommodate future growth.*

Source: Reprinted with permission from the Bartlett Tree Research Laboratories.

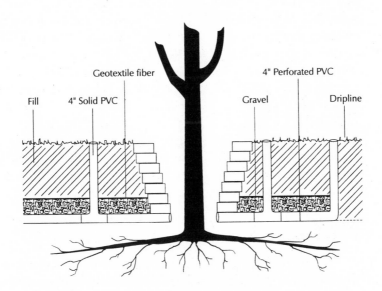

5.6 *When raising the grade around a tree, install a dry well with an aeration system.*

Source: Reprinted with permission from the Bartlett Tree Research Laboratories.

the tree no more than an inch or two, and not at all for small trees. As little as 3 or 4 inches of added soil can smother trees of considerable size and age. A raised grade should begin at the dripline or beyond. Under no circumstances should a retaining wall or tree well come within 3 feet of the trunk.

To raise the soil level or build a tree well, scrape the topsoil clean of grass and organic matter to keep it from compacting into a slick, impervious mat. Then lay down several inches of rounded gravel (angular gravel will settle too much, destroying the porous effect). Cover the gravel layer with geotextile fabric to keep soil from settling and filling in the spaces in the gravel.

There are various methods for providing air to roots. One is to install perforated PVC piping—with holes facing downward—in a network radiating outward horizontally at 45-degree angles from the trunk in the direction of the raised grade (see Figure 5.7). Use PVC piping 2 inches or greater in diameter and install it radiating horizontally outward at 22.5-degree angles for extra insurance. Vertical shafts are added from the gravel layer to the new, higher surface to allow air to pass to the porous gravel layer below.

When installing either the tree well or the retaining wall, it is important not to dig and pour a footing all the way across the root zone. Such trenching will leave at least one side of the tree with its roots cut. The top of the wall or well should rise several inches above the new, higher soil level to prevent rain from washing soil and debris into the pit.

If a tree well is built, consider installing an iron grate at the top to prevent people and animals from falling into the pit. Some local regulations require this. These grates will require regular cleaning, since trash tends to collect in them. It is possible to save trees even when their entire root systems are buried deeper than they were before development. Generally speaking, though, this is so expensive that it is usually preferable either to alter grading plans or consider transplanting the tree.

Utility Installation

As discussed in Chapter 3, when laying water, sewer, gas, or utility lines (electric, telephone, cable TV), it's best to avoid digging in the critical root zone of protected trees. When utility lines must go

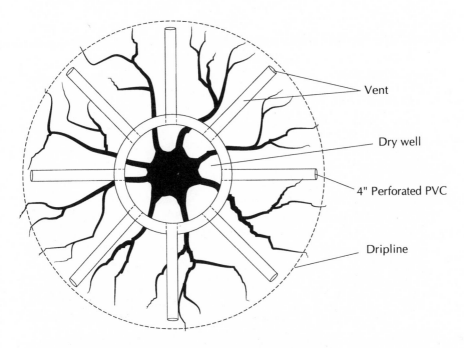

5.7 Plan view of a dry well and aeration system that extends radially around the tree out to the dripline.

Source: Reprinted with permission from the Bartlett Tree Research Laboratories.

through root zones, tunneling under roots is preferable to trenching. This technique is expensive, so as a practical matter, tunneling is typically used with specimen trees or for projects such as street widenings in already built areas with large established trees. When tunneling is warranted and feasible, dig the tunnel at least 2 feet deep, although 3 feet or more is best. Avoid the top 18 inches of soil altogether. Trees in light, sandy soils may have many roots that go even deeper.

Hand labor is often used and sometimes specified by local regulations. Specialized equipment, such as a vibratory plow or a rock chisel, will also do a good job because they cut roots cleanly. As discussed in Chapter 4, other ways to avoid widespread root damage include using a single tunnel or trench or a shared corridor to combine several utilities.

Building

At the building stage, the amount of ground space available for walking, driving, and storing materials dwindles rapidly. Global Re-Leaf for New Communities award recipient United Parcel Service (UPS) actually set tower cranes inside its building footprints during the early stages of construction instead of clearing crane sites outside the building area. This made it possible to use the large equipment necessary to build commercial buildings, while preserving trees that were in some cases only 15 feet away.

During construction, applications of paint or stain, especially oil-based products, can harm trees, soil, wildlife, and water resources. When spraying or painting these products onto exterior surfaces, spread plastic sheeting on the ground to catch the drips—particularly for work done beyond the housing-pad shelf (for example, staining a deck). Remove plastic sheeting immediately to keep it from trapping solar radiation as heat, harming soils and the feeder roots of trees and shrubs. For an alternative to plastic, lay a 12-inch layer of wood chips over root zones.

Hardscape Installation

The street-paving process rarely poses new hazards to saved trees, since it occurs on already graded land. Driveways are another matter, as retained trees are often closer to driveways than to streets. Consult with the natural resource expert to carefully locate driveways in such cases.

It is essential, of course, that any subcontractors pouring concrete use the designated washout zones to clean trucks and equipment (see Figure 5.8). The arrival, storage, and preparation of paving materials, and the heavy equipment associated with them, should take place outside root protection zones. Even fumes and radiant heat from asphalt cookers can damage nearby or overhead trees and branches.

As soon as streets and other surfaces are paved, runoff increases, making less water available for absorption on-site by trees and other vegetation. Impervious surfaces will radiate more heat into the air, making the air hotter and drier. Therefore, it is vital to pay careful attention to the watering needs of existing trees and

5.8 Designate special concrete washout areas to avoid chemical contamination of soil and vegetation.

Source: Reprinted with permission from the Michael T. Rose Consulting Company, Inc., Laurel, Maryland.

greenscape. If construction takes place during summer or with summer just ahead, the heat stress on plants is even greater.

Landscaping

In most instances, the irrigation system and related utilities for landscaping are not installed along with the other utilities. To keep from disturbing roots, install them before any new or transplanted trees, shrubs, or flowers are introduced to the site. Any amending of soils (including forced-air treatment to loosen compacted soil) or returning of stockpiled native topsoil follows.

The next step is to install the new plant material. Larger tree specimens are planted first; regardless of size, place trees into the landscape before shrubs and flowers. The root zones of newly planted trees, though smaller than those of preserved trees, require an equal amount of attention throughout the remainder of construction.

Larger shrubs follow the trees, then smaller shrubs and flowers. Water trees, even if there is a delay between when they are planted and other materials are added. In fact, plants should not sit dry while other materials are being worked in. It is best to water the site gently, then add mulch and water again. If mulch is added before watering, it may soak up most or all of the water.

In the Field

No matter how thorough the planning, no matter how good the development team and the construction crews, problems will arise in the field when construction is underway. Unexpected problems or discrepancies between what's shown on the drawings and actual field conditions may require minor—and sometimes major—adjustments to roads, driveways, or buildings.

Even a developer experienced in tree conservation will want to have the natural resource expert on call for such situations. In land development, last-minute adjustments in the field are simply a part of life. The developer who has retained his or her natural resource expert will have not only peace of mind, but a greater chance of achieving a successful project that meets the development goals.

The Need for a "Hammer"—A Penalty Clause

Communication is key to the successful implementation of development plans. All players in the construction process must understand the plans and goals set by the developer, natural resource expert, and design team and agree to participate in their fulfillment. No developer should have a crew begin work without obtaining this expressed commitment.

However, a developer committed to conservation goals will almost certainly need something stronger than goodwill to fall back on to ensure goals are met. An enforcement or penalty clause in the builder's and general contractor's contracts should establish a structure of punitive fines for violating tree protection zones, injuring roots or above-ground portions of trees, using improper grading techniques, or failing to follow other protective measures spelled out in the tree conservation element of the master plan.

Fines provide a strong incentive for strict adherence to the construction plans and offer the developer some financial recourse in case an on-site error ruins a significant portion of the plan. Fines also establish the authority of the natural resource expert, who can halt construction if trees are damaged or the tree conservation plan is not followed. In some cases, too, a municipality reserves the right to fine the developer for damage to trees or other natural features, so a penalty clause protects the developer somewhat. And potential fines can be the incentive that makes the difference between status quo work and a team's best efforts.

Developers must carry out punitive actions if violations occur or risk having contractors and others perceive their tree conservation goals as unimportant. Assess appropriate penalties promptly. The experience UPS had in building its corporate headquarters in Atlanta, Georgia, bears out the need for and the effectiveness of penalties. UPS committed itself to building with the environment on this site, and its efforts included a major road rerouted to avoid catastrophic root damage to a large tulip poplar and a 50-inch utility line laid in a costly zigzag formation to avoid an impressive stand of oaks.

UPS had committed itself financially to protecting its tree resources and took no chances on damage during construction. Contractors had to sign a special document stating they had learned UPS's tree preservation goals and agreed to comply with them. However, damage occurred early on during grading. While some might have thought the damage minor, penalties were levied. The penalty structure was calculated based on tree size, species, condition, location, diameter, and the percentage that was damaged, using as a reference the *Guide for Plant Appraisal* by the Council of Tree & Landscape Appraisers. As a result of this enforcement approach, no further damage occurred.

This incident affirms the value of having carefully communicated—in writing—the project's tree conservation goals and penalties and the importance of having contractors and subcontractors sign off on them. The developer must levy fines promptly when damage or other violations occur and move quickly to settle the incident so that work resumes immediately.

Long-Term Site Management and Maintenance

Regardless of whether a developer builds homes on the lots or sells the finished lots to other home builders, he or she will want to ensure that tree conservation efforts continue. Several mechanisms can ensure that the development team's environmental goals carry through to the construction and sale of homes. Some apply to the home-building process, others to long-term care by home buyers.

Influencing the Builder

To keep goals—and trees—alive through the building process, the developer should begin by selecting qualified professionals. Many developers find it essential to educate builders about the economic benefits of protecting existing trees near homes. Just as subcontractors did during the land development phase, builders and their subcontractors should have to sign off on specified standards to further ensure quality.

Global ReLeaf for New Communities award recipient David Gale implemented several mechanisms for ensuring that tree conservation techniques continued in his Winterset Park development in Lee's Summit, Missouri:

- All builders were educated about the benefits of saving trees.
- Gale's company, F.E.L. Lands, maintained review rights over the placement of homes on each lot and flagged trees or groups of trees that were not to be disturbed during construction.
- F.E.L. Lands reserved the right to determine the transplant potential of trees within building footprints and maintained rights to trees slated for destruction, if they were suitable for transplanting.
- Builders were required to pay a variable compliance deposit based on lot size ($1,000 minimum) and a penalty of $100 per diameter inch if trees were damaged.

Developer Gale notes that he can impose such requirements because of the strength of his share in the local market, a position he believes he has achieved by creating a quality development with mature trees. While not all developers claim such specific controls, many reserve the right to have their natural resource expert regularly inspect lots throughout the building process and again at the end of construction. Before construction begins, agreement is reached on what actions the developer will take if a contractor damages trees or other resources.

Developers can also impose certain design guidelines and limitations on builders, such as requiring them to review plans with the natural resource expert; to minimize cut and fill; to coordinate utility installation so root disturbance is minimized; to use pier rather than slab foundations; or to alter the elevation, footprint, or location of the house to maximize tree retention.

The reward for a developer who creates lots with healthy, attractive trees is price, appeal, and demand. Builders wishing to buy from or work with such a developer will usually see the benefits of this approach and carry through with the developer's quality goals—particularly if these goals have been communicated and carry an incentive for compliance.

Before the Sale

Once construction is winding down, there are still a few details to work out before the final sale. Dispose of debris left on the construction site, as it can harm trees. (Remember developer C.P. Morgan's donation of scrap wood to a local environmental group. Contact the NAHB Environmental Regulations Department for information about recycling construction site waste.) Once construction has ceased and debris is gone, remove protective fences from tree protection areas. Protective fencing must stay in place until this point.

The natural resource expert or a qualified landscape professional conducts the final site inspection. During this inspection, trees are checked for injury, signs of stress, and elements that could influence tree health. A significantly damaged tree might already demonstrate dieback and other signs of decline. If trees have suffered injury, they need professional treatment. If root damage caused the decline, removal may be the only option.

The natural resource expert may recommend that preserved and transplanted trees receive watering, pruning, mulching, or fertilizing. Specimen trees and significant trees within groupings also are candidates for lightning protection.

Reaching the Home Buyer

Home buyers must also know about the long-term maintenance of trees. Some developers set up protective covenants or deed restrictions that ensure long-term protection and care. Others establish contracts with professional landscaping firms for maintenance of common areas, gradually turning these over to the homeowners' association as the development is built-out, but leaving maintenance of individual homesites as the responsibility of homeowners. At a minimum, it's a good idea to provide educational materials about tree care to home buyers and to remind them that the trees are a valuable asset to the community and to themselves (see Figure 5.9). Developer C.P. Morgan finds that sales staff can sell home buyers on the value of trees before homes are built. Home buyers then become more interested in the long-term value of their lots and more watchful of builders as the homes go up.

Protective Covenants. Protective covenants are protection agreements created by the development company and attached to the property deed. They were rarely used to ensure tree protection a few years ago but are becoming more common. Until build-out, the developer usually retains review and control of design details through an architectural review committee that is part of the homeowners' association. Once a community is built-out, this review function is turned over to the homeowners' association.

5.9 Educational materials can provide home buyers with the information they need to care for trees on their property and can explain the value of these community assets.

Source: Reprinted with permission from the Michael T. Rose Consulting Company, Inc., Laurel, Maryland.

The best tree protection covenants allow flexibility in home design and siting. Protective covenants may contain provisions allowing the removal of trees under specific circumstances, such as when trees die or become diseased, when growth threatens a foundation or other essential constructed element, or when the trees are in the way of an approved addition. Landscape easements written into property deeds in a number of developer C.P. Morgan's communities prevent homeowners from cutting trees in rear yards where trees have been retained.

Violating the terms of a covenant—by damaging or destroying a protected tree—may result in a fine or other penalty for the responsible party. Many covenants specify that if a tree wound proves fatal or a tree is removed, it must be replaced by another tree of similar value. Base fines on realistic and current landscape values, just as with the fine structure established for contractors. Publish the fine structure as part of the covenant the home buyer signs. Protective covenants do more than ensure that the developer's careful planning and work are protected over the long term. They also serve as a marketing tool, assuring potential home buyers that the natural character of their neighborhood will grow rather than decline.

Professional Maintenance Contracts. Some of the natural areas retained on a site will require maintenance only to address hazards from fallen trees or limbs. The homeowners' association will also need to contract for regular, long-term professional landscape maintenance of common areas. Annual homeowners' dues can help finance this continuing effort. The natural resource expert is familiar with the horticultural aspects of the property and can often advise the landscape maintenance firm on its needs and peculiarities. Another option is to hire an on-site landscape maintenance employee, just as employees are hired to handle other routine maintenance jobs.

More Protection Through Education. One of the best ways to ensure that homeowners understand their role in maintaining trees in their community and don't undo a developer's environmental accomplishments is to provide educational materials at the time of sale. Some developers, such as C.P. Morgan, include tree care information in their company or community newsletters to reach homeowners on an ongoing basis. Even in neighborhoods with healthy trees, homeowners need reminders about such basics as checking and, as necessary, removing stakes from newly planted trees.

AMERICAN FORESTS publishes the *Tree Care Checklist*, a free booklet that gives general information about planting and caring for trees. Several Global ReLeaf for New Communities award recipients have published the *Checklist* in their home buyer's manuals or have offered copies to new homeowners. More detailed information about tree care can be found in *Growing Greener Cities*, AMERICAN FORESTS' urban forestry handbook, and in *Urban Forests* and *American Forests* magazines, available by subscription from the organization (see Appendix).

Many other organizations, including the National Arborists Association, the International Society of Arboriculture, and the U.S. Department of Agriculture Forest Service, offer publications and brochures of varying detail and complexity. For specific information on local species and climate, contact the county extension service or the state Department of Forestry. In addition, the American Association of Nurserymen (AAN) and AMERICAN FORESTS have published a guide to selecting nursery stock in volume (*Selecting Trees: A Guide to Purchasing Quality Trees as a Wise Investment*, see Appendix).

Distress Signals

Maintaining healthy trees is the goal during construction. However, even with extraordinary care and effort, a new development that saves many of the site's existing trees can expect to see some casualties. The highest success rate reported to AMERICAN FORESTS for tree survival in developments is about 90 percent.

Open spaces, streets, and buildings will create windy zones that can desiccate and damage trees. Hardscape and drainage systems mean less available soil moisture—at least from natural sources—which can add new stress to roots. If the development is sited where a forest once stood, any introduction of grass is always a shock to the remaining trees, since grass is highly competitive for moisture and nutrients. Combining these and other factors with any actual damage done to roots, trunks, or limbs will almost certainly affect some trees and may kill others.

Most of these trees will die slowly. Home buyers should know how to spot symptoms of distress in trees and where to turn for help (see Figure 5.10). A developer can help by providing telephone numbers for the natural resource expert or International Society of Arboriculture-certified tree care professionals. Since the resource expert is already intimately acquainted with the particular site and its tree species, this approach makes excellent sense.

Getting the Bugs Out. Stressed trees attract insect pests through released chemicals and occasionally through high-pitched sounds that are inaudible to humans. Discoloration of leaves and branches may also attract insects. With the exception of gypsy moth caterpillars and elm bark beetles, few chewing insects pose a

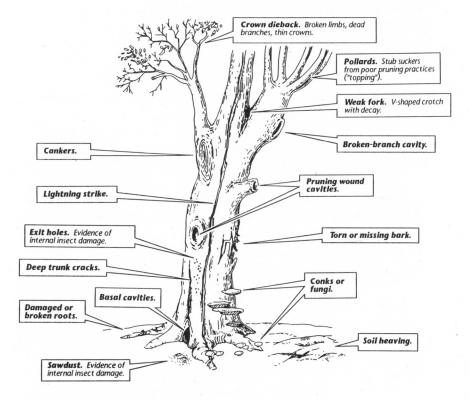

5.10 Visual clues of a tree in distress.

Source: Drawing is copyrighted by, and reproduced with the permission of, the Minnesota Extension Service, University of Minnesota, from its publication FO-6135, *Protecting Trees from Construction Damage* (revised 1995).

lethal hazard to healthy trees. However, homeowners should watch stressed trees closely for chewed leaves and stems; these trees may not have the energy to leaf out again if defoliated. A qualified arborist should examine the tree if the homeowner is in doubt or insects have attacked a stressed tree.

Since hole-boring insects are serious threats, a tree with damaged bark requires close monitoring. Call a specialist at the first sign of holes. The appearance of powdered bark or sawdust in the bark or at the base of the tree is a clear danger signal. Some trees, including pines, gums, and certain oaks, bleed sap profusely at wounds, an indication of serious or ongoing injuries.

Sucking insects can be extremely difficult to spot. Homeowners should know to watch for new growth that, though green, is curled or stunted. Close examination will probably reveal the culprits attracted to the tender new growth. Another common sign of sucking insects is profuse mildew that "blackens" leaves and branches.

Integrated Pest Management. Scientists now recognize that managing insects, weeds, rodents, and plant diseases is a complex science. With concern growing about the effects of pesticides on human health, public agencies and private practitioners have recognized the need for more safe, efficient, and effective ways of controlling pests. This understanding has evolved into a new pest management strategy called integrated pest management (IPM).

IPM prevents and suppresses pests using techniques that minimize the impact on human health, noninvasive organisms, and the environment. IPM requires a thorough understanding of pests' life histories, growth requirements, and natural enemies and adopts a system of regular monitoring for the presence of pests.

IPM techniques include selecting plant species and cultivars that resist pests; adopting landscape maintenance practices such as pruning, fertilizing, and irrigation that reduce pest problems; monitoring pest and disease life cycles; changing the habitat to make it incompatible with pest proliferation; and using natural biological controls. Broad-spectrum pesticides are used as a last resort when preestablished guidelines and careful monitoring indicate they are warranted. When this is necessary, select the least toxic, target-specific pesticides available.

Homeowners need to understand the practice of IPM so they know, for example, not to kill brightly colored ladybugs or green lacewings. (Incidentally, the electric blue "bug lights" some homeowners put out have been found to kill as many or more beneficial insects as harmful ones.) Homeowners can help monitor for signs of pests, but it's best to have an arborist come in periodically, since IPM works best when trouble is caught early on.

At present, IPM cannot completely replace chemical pest control, but it is an excellent option for many pest problems. Growing public concern with and government regulation of the use of toxic chemicals, coupled with rising prices, will only make IPM more attractive in the future.

The Fungus Among Us. In addition to insect problems, stressed trees are more prone to an array of fungal, bacterial, and viral diseases. Again, the best way to prevent disease outbreaks is to keep trees healthy by following the steps already described in this book. Bacterial and viral diseases usually enter through wounds. Viral infection, though uncommon, is incurable, and an infected tree can contaminate any other trees with which it has physical contact. Both connected roots and tree-cutting tools that are not disinfected after use are easy conduits for disease. Viruses can remain in soil for years.

Many homeowners find variegated plants attractive, but few realize that some types of variegation are caused by plant viruses. (Other types are caused by a plant's genes.) The white or yellow patches on leaves lack chlorophyll and make a plant weaker than its solid green companions. Disinfect thoroughly any equipment used to prune or dig around these plants.

If a tree's previously solid green leaves become variegated, the cause is viral infection. Viruses can also disfigure leaves and deform or mottle flowers. Other viruses "vanish" into the plant, producing no visible symptoms. Whenever a plant is removed because it is thought to have a viral infection, be sure the soil it was in is sterilized or replaced. The natural resource expert will know the steps necessary for soil sterilization, which requires either chemicals or heat.

Bacterial infection is the principal cause of heart rot, which can strike any tree. Heart rot begins with any wound that collects water; bacteria breed in the water and rot the wood. (Remember, the heartwood of a tree is not living tissue.) Heart rot is difficult or impossible to stop, necessitating a call to the natural resource expert. Again, the case is made for preventing wounds to trees rather than curing them.

Wilts are caused by fungi and account for some of the most serious pest problems faced by trees in this country. Chestnut blight, oak wilt, Dutch elm disease, dogwood anthracnose, fire blight, citrus canker, and avocado root rot are all fungal diseases. Sometimes, as in the case of Dutch elm disease, they are spread by insect pests. Control programs must take into account both the disease and the mode of infection transmission.

Wilts and blights often cause a rapid decline in a tree's health. Leaves and tender stems may yellow, then die, or may darken and shrivel in short order; in either case, death is quick—almost always within a single season. A homeowner who sees a tree go into rapid decline should know to call for expert help immediately. Some wilts and blights, such as fire blight, can be controlled with sprays. Oak wilt, a problem both in the North—with red oaks—and in the Southwest—with live oaks—can sometimes be halted with root pruning and soil removal. Prompt removal and disposal is required once a tree has died from disease. The natural resource expert may need to prescribe a soil treatment or spray program for surrounding vegetation, depending on the disease.

Be Wary of Weed Trimmers. Homeowners often unintentionally inflict a particular hazard on their own trees: lawn mowers and weed trimmers. Often, the only trees in a development that are protected by mulch are the ones planted during landscaping. The rest are usually left with no barrier against grass trimmers. Trees with grass growing right up to their trunks are particularly vulnerable. Lawn mowers and weed trimmers open wounds in the bark and kill the tissue layers underneath. Since the phloem layer directly beneath the bark is the transport area for energy (see Chapter 3), it cuts off the tree's lifeline. Trees that don't desiccate, starve, or "bleed" to death are left vulnerable to insects and disease.

Buried Alive. Homeowners also may not realize that those attractive raised flowerbeds around their trees can kill the trees. As with grading, a rise in the soil level of only a few inches can smother the roots of even large trees. The baffled homeowner, seeing wilting, assumes the trees simply need more frequent watering, which only hastens death in this case because it closes up the few air holes left in the soil.

Remodeling

A remodeling or home improvement project can affect backyard trees. Protective covenants go part of the way toward addressing this, but not every community has a protective covenant. In non-covenanted communities, developers should inform home buyers about how future remodeling can affect trees. The basic principles are the same for remodeling as for new construction. Advised of even a few facts—such as the dangers of changing soil levels around trees or cutting major roots—homeowners can then seek out a natural resource expert or an ISA-certified arborist.

Conclusion

By helping builders, subcontractors, and homeowners understand what injures or stresses trees, the developer completes the final link of care in a chain of events that allows people and trees to happily coexist in a community. The final chapter of this book explains how developers and builders can market their efforts at building in concert with the environment and how they can receive recognition for a job well done.

Chapter 6

Recognition for a Job Well Done

Most people like recognition for a job well done. Developers are no different. As environmental awareness among the home-buying public has grown, more developers have begun working in harmony with the natural features of the land, earning praise from citizen groups and public officials for their efforts.

In 1992, the C.P. Morgan Company received the Forest Conservationist Award from the Indiana Wildlife Federation for its Lake Forest development. David Yost was designated 1994 Conservationist of the Year by the Oklahoma Chapter of the Soil and Water Conservation Society for his tree protection and planting efforts. Michael T. Rose's communities have accumulated numerous awards, among them the Chesapeake Bay Conservation Award from the Izaak Walton League of America. As previously mentioned, one of his developments was even designated an Urban Wildlife Sanctuary by the National Institute for Urban Wildlife.

Until 1991, however, award opportunities at the national level were limited. In 1990, AMERICAN FORESTS posed a simple question to members and staff of the National Association of Home Builders: "Why aren't more trees saved during development?" NAHB explained that local regulatory requirements often force developers and builders to remove some trees and that, while many were interested in retaining and planting more trees, they were not receiving the necessary technical information to do this successfully.

Because developers and builders also received little recognition or public support when they did conserve trees, AMERICAN FORESTS and NAHB decided to jointly sponsor a program both to offer this recognition and to make information available on protecting trees during construction. The program was envisioned as a way to inform the public and local officials about development success stories and the cooperative efforts that made them possible.

The new recognition program—Global ReLeaf for New Communities—is an outgrowth of AMERICAN FORESTS' Global ReLeaf campaign, a worldwide tree conservation and planting effort. The philosophy and goals of the New Communities program serve as the basis for this book. Global ReLeaf for New Communities assists and rewards developers who save, plant, and transplant trees and who work in concert with the land's natural features (see Figure 6.1).

The guidelines for participating in Global ReLeaf for New Communities ensure quality while allowing some flexibility. Developers may send in their initial registration at any time but may submit a development for final review only when the project is at least 75 percent complete. The reason: New Communities recognition is based on how well a developer integrates trees into the completed project. (For a program brochure and registration forms, write to AMERICAN FORESTS, P.O. Box 2000, Washington, DC 20013.)

The review process itself is a collaborative effort between AMERICAN FORESTS and NAHB. Qualified staff from the two organizations make up

6.1 The Global ReLeaf for New Communities program nationally recognizes developers and builders who conserve trees and work in concert with the land's natural features.

Source: AMERICAN FORESTS and NAHB.

a review panel, which examines each development's unique elements. Some of the elements considered include the following:

♦ The trees—what the development team had to work with on-site, how development plans incorporated this resource, and what the regional norms and constraints are.

♦ Other natural resources—how the developer or builder protected and/or used waterways, ridges, open space, and existing topography.

♦ The construction process—what accommodations were made in the grading and the siting of utilities, streets, and parking areas; what protective techniques and materials were used throughout the development and construction process.

♦ The development as built—how well the development's overall design and layout achieved program objectives.

Variability of sites and approaches is also considered. Both AMERICAN FORESTS and NAHB recognize that not all sites start out well treed and that not all trees are worth saving. Regional factors (such as arid Western climate and water needs) are also taken into account. Predevelopment site conditions on qualifying projects to date have ranged from magnificent hardwood groves to gullied, largely bare pastureland.

Though the program has high standards, all developments following the guidelines can expect to receive the prestigious Global ReLeaf for New Communities designation—there is no single, grand award. There is also no limit to the number of properties that may receive the New Communities designation in any given year.

Global ReLeaf Program Benefits

In addition to national recognition, the Global ReLeaf for New Communities designation offers recipients some very specific benefits. Developments designated as Global ReLeaf New Communities are widely promoted through AMERICAN FORESTS' and NAHB's press releases, publications, and conferences. Press releases distributed in the developer's local area ensure hometown recognition, and features in two of the organizations' magazines provide national exposure. Professional publications also pick up the press releases.

Winners are honored at NAHB's annual convention and at AMERICAN FORESTS' biannual National Urban Forest Conference (and its fall meeting in nonconference years). Designees are entitled to use the Global ReLeaf for New Communities name and logo to promote their award-winning project, and they may also purchase promotional site signs from AMERICAN FORESTS (see Figure 6.2) and receive informational brochures on tree care to pass on to homeowners.

Perhaps the most important benefit, winners say, is an enhanced public image at the state and local levels. Many of the winning developments have received numerous write-ups in local newspapers. Roger Gatewood of Westfield Development Corporation has said, "The Global ReLeaf for New Communities award has brought us a new and significant level of credibility with land sellers, municipalities, and the media. It has opened up doors for us throughout the community."

Receiving New Community designation for a project helps developers stand out from the crowd in their market area and provides a public relations benefit that, as Gatewood put it, cannot be bought at any price. This enhanced image affects everything from the developer's ability to obtain permits and waivers to the privilege of bidding for choice prop-

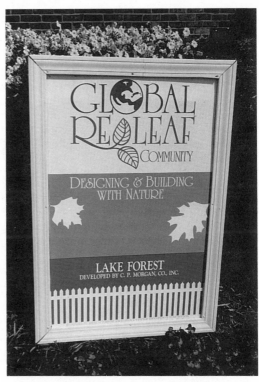

6.2 Global ReLeaf for New Communities signage promotes award-winning projects.

Source: Reprinted with permission from the C.P. Morgan Company.

erties from environmentally sensitive sellers. The home building industry at large also benefits from the positive press the program generates and from the resulting success stories that can be promoted nationally.

New Communities participants also say their developments sell better than the norm for their local market—even during soft market periods. This is because receiving the New Communities designation helps create more salable properties that reflect the concerns of home buyers today. The program provides developers with the latest urban forestry technology and pairs them with skilled natural resource experts. These experts can help obtain local planning approvals, increase public support, make sure the techniques employed on a site do in fact conserve trees, and help developers understand the ways the natural environment can work successfully with the built one. Based not just on good science but on good economics as well, Global ReLeaf for New Communities works for developers *and* for the communities in which they build.

Marketing Success

With or without an award, developers can feature their more natural communities in their marketing materials. Remember, surveys show that home buyers like bike paths, hiking trails, mature trees, and ponds close to home. Sales brochures and other promotional materials used in marketing new homes in a development can showcase these amenities and appeal to that interest.

Michael T. Rose has been conserving trees in his developments for more than 20 years and uses a tree as his company logo. His corporate slogan is "Creating Communities That Live With Nature." Newspaper advertisements for his communities include their trees, lakes, wildlife, and nature trails, enticing buyers to come and take a look (see Figure 6.3).

Holding tours or a tree-planting event on-site for local officials or school children can also attract attention. AMERICAN FORESTS can provide information on how to participate in its Famous & Historic Trees planting program for such events. C.P. Morgan's monthly newsletters for home buyers frequently highlight the natural amenities the company retained and enhanced in its communities, such as the arboretum and walking trail at Lake Forest. C.P. Morgan, Michael T. Rose, David Gale, and others also prepare nature guides that describe the trees, flowers, and wildlife species that can be found in their communities. Pamphlets like these are distributed at the sales center or provided to home buyers at the final sale along with fact sheets on tree care.

Conclusion

Builders and developers are in a unique position to shape the land and infrastructure in our communities. Many have already pioneered techniques for designing with the land and conserving more trees. The success stories described in this book show that these alternative development and construction methods are not only possible but valuable. Today's home buyers

6.3 Developers can feature their more natural communities in marketing materials, appealing to home buyers' interest in these amenities.

Source: Reprinted with permission from the Michael T. Rose Consulting Company, Inc., Laurel, Maryland.

seek more than just a house on a lot, they seek a home in a livable community with natural amenities—and they have shown they are willing to pay for it. By saving, planting, and transplanting trees, developers and builders can deliver such neighborhoods.

Successful tree conservation requires a shared vision and a commitment from all those involved in creating a new development: from the members of the development team, to local government officials, to the home buyers—local citizens—who eventually become the stewards of the developer's and builder's vision. When trees are made part of the plan, we all contribute to and benefit from building greener neighborhoods.

Appendix

Other Resources

American Association of Nurserymen (AAN)
1250 I Street, NW, Suite 500
Washington, DC 20005
(202) 789-2900; (202) 789-1893 (fax)

Publications: *American Standard for Nursery Stock.*

AMERICAN FORESTS
P.O. Box 2000
Washington, DC 20013-2000
(202) 667-3300; (202) 667-7751 (fax)

Programs: Global ReLeaf for New Communities recognition program
(contact AMERICAN FORESTS for program information and a developer registration form, for a list of natural resource experts, or to apply
for natural resource expert certification); Global ReLeaf; Famous & Historic Trees.

Publications: *Shading Our Cities,* edited by Gary Moll and Sara Ebenreck; *Growing Greener Cities,* Gary Moll and Stanley Young; *Selecting
Trees: A Guide to Purchasing Quality Trees as a Wise Investment,* Cheryl
Kollin and Jeff Pappas; *Knowing Your Trees,* G.H. Collingwood and War-
ren Brush; *Tree Care Checklist* (for homeowners); *Urban Forests* magazine; *American Forests* magazine.

American Planning Association (APA)
122 South Michigan Avenue, Suite 1600
Chicago, IL 60603-6107
(312) 431-9100; (312) 431-9985 (fax)

Publications: *Environment & Development* newsletter; *APA Journal; Planning* magazine; *Tree Conservation Ordinances,* Christopher J. Duerksen and Suzanne Richman; *Rural by Design,* Randall Arendt.

American Society of Consulting Arborists
5130 West 101st Circle
Westminster, CO 80030
(303) 466-2722; (303) 466-7401 (fax)

Publications: *Arboriculture Consultant.*

American Society of Landscape Architects (ASLA)
4401 Connecticut Avenue, NW, Fifth Floor
Washington, DC 20008-2369
(202) 686-2752; (202) 686-1001 (fax)

Publications: *Landscape Architecture* magazine; *Landscape Architecture News Digest;* listing of landscape architects by state.

Council of Tree & Landscape Appraisers
5130 West 101st Circle
Westminster, CO 80030
(303) 466-7657

International Society of Arboriculture (ISA)
P.O. Box GG
Savoy, IL 61874
(217) 355-9411; (217) 355-9516 (fax)

Publications: *Journal of Arboriculture; Tree Care Bulletins;* listing of ISA-certified arborists.

Municipal Arborists and Urban Foresters Society
P.O. Box 1255
Freehold, NJ 07728-1255
(908) 431-7903

National Arbor Day Foundation
100 Arbor Avenue
Nebraska City, NE 68410
(402) 474-5655; (402) 474-0820 (fax)

Publications: *Tree City USA Bulletins; Arbor Day News.*

National Arborists Association, Inc. (NAA)
P.O. Box 1094
Amherst, NH 03031
(603) 673-3311; (603) 672-2613 (fax)

Publications: *Standard Practices for Trees, Shrubs and Other Woody Plant Maintenance, ANSI 300; National Arborists Reporter; Tree Worker.*

National Association of Home Builders
1201 15th Street, NW
Washington, DC 20005-2800
(202) 822-0200; (202) 822-0391 (fax)

Programs: Global ReLeaf for New Communities recognition program.

Publications: *Land Development* magazine; *Land Development, Eighth Edition,* D. Linda Kone; *Site Planning and Community Design for Great Neighborhoods,* Frederick D. Jarvis; *Land Buying Checklist, Fourth Edition,* Ralph M. Lewis.

References

ARBOR National Mortgage, Inc. "Realtors Agree Trees Enhance Property Value." News Release, New York, April 19, 1994.

Bartlett Tree Expert Co. "Roots (Part Four)." *Tree Tips,* vol. 11, no. 2 (Winter 1993).

Bassuk, Nina. "Urban Trees." *Proceedings of the Sixth National Urban Forest Conference.* Washington, DC: AMERICAN FORESTS, 1994.

Britton, John C. *Tree Protection Specifications.* St. Helena, CA: John Britton Tree Service, 1989.

City of New York Department of Parks & Recreation. *DPR Street Tree Preservation, Protection and Planting Standards.* New York, April 26, 1990.

Clark, Earl. "Pests That Attack City Trees." *Urban Forests,* vol. 12, no. 3 (June/July 1992).

Clark, James R., and Nelda P. Matheny. "Tree Retention: Rooted in Good Planning?" *Environment & Development,* June 1994.

Clark, Steve. "Saving Trees on Construction Sites." *Journal of Arboriculture,* vol. 16, no. 1 (January 1990), pp. 8-11.

Coder, Kim D. "How Trees Make a Living: Tree Biology." *Proceedings of the Sixth National Urban Forest Conference.* Washington, DC: AMERICAN FORESTS, 1994.

Council of Tree & Landscape Appraisers. *Guide for Plant Appraisal,* 8th ed. Savoy, IL: International Society of Arboriculture, 1992.

Duerksen, Christopher J., and Suzanne Richman. *Tree Conservation Ordinances.* Washington, DC: American Planning Association and Scenic America, 1993.

Ebenreck, Sara. "Measuring the Values of Trees." *American Forests,* vol. 94, nos. 7 & 8 (July/August 1988).

Fazio, James R., Ph.D. *Trenching & Tunneling Near Trees: A Field Pocket Guide for Qualified Utility Workers.* Nebraska City, NE: National Arbor Day Foundation, 1992.

Fraedrich, Bruce R., Ph.D. "Managing Mature Trees." *Tree Topics,* Winter 1994, p. 4.

"How Can Builders Help the Environment?" *Builder,* vol. 17, no. 6 (May 1994), p. 43.

How to Care for Trees During Construction (a course designed for Realen Homes, Inc.). Philadelphia: The Morris Arboretum of the University of Pennsylvania, 1993.

Hull, R. Bruce, and Roger S. Ulrich. "Health Benefits and Costs of Urban Trees." *Proceedings of the Fifth National Urban Forestry Conference.* Washington, DC: American Forestry Association, 1992.

Koehler, C.S., R.H. Hunt, D.F. Lobel, and J. Geiger. "Protecting Trees when Building on Forested Land." Richmond, CA: University of California, Cooperative Extension, 1984.

Kollin, Cheryl. " 'Cycling' Through the Urban Ecosystem." *Urban Forests,* vol. 14, no. 5 (October/November 1994).

Leach, Carolyn B. "Evaluating Construction Plans for Impacts on Trees." *Journal of Arboriculture,* vol. 20, no. 1 (January 1994), pp. 55-60.

Macie, Ed. "Characteristics of a Model Tree Protection and Landscaping Ordinance." *Proceedings of the Fourth National Urban Forestry Conference.* Washington, DC: American Forestry Association, 1989.

Michael T. Rose Chartered Co. *Northridge: A Community That Lives with Nature.* Laurel, MD, 1988.

Miller, Nancy L., David M. Rathke, and Gary R. Johnson. *Protecting Trees from Construction Damage: A Homeowner's Guide.* Saint Paul: University of Minnesota, Minnesota Extension Service, 1993.

Moll, Gary. "Creative Construction: (Or, How the Do-It-Yourselfer Can Avoid Killing Trees)." *American Forests,* vol. 91, no. 7 (July 1985).

Moll, Gary, and Stanley Young. *Growing Greener Cities.* Venice, CA: Living Planet Press and American Forestry Association, 1992.

National Association of Home Builders, Economics Department. "Builders Surveyed on Environmental Issues." Washington, DC, 1994.

Olsen, Jean E., and Paul H. Wray. "Preventing Construction Damage to Trees." Ames, IA: Iowa State University, Cooperative Extension Service, 1986.

Perry, Thomas O., and Gary Hennen. "The Forest Underground." *Shading Our Cities.* Washington, DC: American Forestry Association, 1989.

Rodbell, Phillip. "A Slice of Life." *Urban Forests,* vol. 13, no. 1 (February/March 1993).

Rodbell, Phillip, Greg McPherson, and Jim Geiger. "Planting the Urban Desert." *Urban Forests,* vol. 11, no. 3 (June/July 1991).

Sand, Peggy. "Design and Species Selection to Reduce Urban Heat Island and Conserve Energy." *Proceedings of the Sixth National Urban Forest Conference.* Washington, DC: AMERICAN FORESTS, 1994.

Schroeder, Herbert, and Charles Lewis. "Psychological Benefits and Costs of Urban Forests." *Proceedings of the Fifth National Urban Forestry Conference.* Washington, DC: American Forestry Association, 1992.

Semrau, Anne. "Helping Trees Weather Nature." *Urban Forests,* vol. 13, no. 1 (February/March 1993).

Semrau, Anne. "Planting & Painting the Town." *Urban Forests,* vol. 12, no. 4 (August/September 1992).

Shigo, Alex A. "Journey to the Center of a Tree." *American Forests,* vol. 92, no. 6 (June 1986).

United Parcel Service. UPS Headquarters Campus Submission for Global Re-Leaf Recognition. Atlanta, GA, 1994.

Watson, Gary W., and Gary Hennen. "Journey to the Bottom of a Tree." *American Forests,* vol. 95, nos. 9 & 10 (September/October 1989).

Wolfe Mason Associates. *City of Sacramento Urban Forest Management Plan.* Sacramento, CA: Draft Plan, January 31, 1992.

Young, Stanley. "The Pest Defense: Knowing Your Quarry." *Urban Forests,* vol. 12, no. 3 (June/July 1992).